The Cambridge Manuals of Science and
Literature

ANCIENT ASSYRIA

HUMAN-HEADED BULL COLOSSUS.

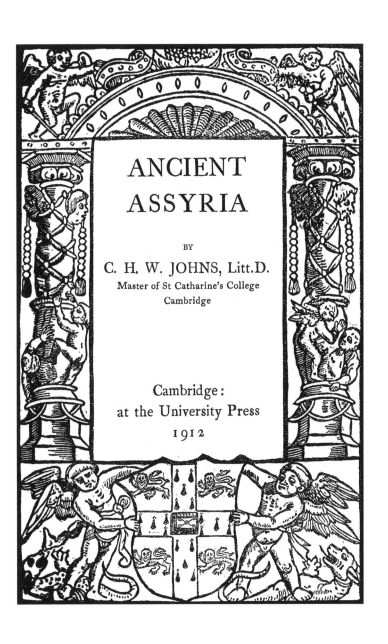

ANCIENT ASSYRIA

BY

C. H. W. JOHNS, Litt.D.

Master of St Catharine's College
Cambridge

Cambridge:
at the University Press
1912

CAMBRIDGE UNIVERSITY PRESS
Cambridge, New York, Melbourne, Madrid, Cape Town,
Singapore, São Paulo, Delhi, Mexico City

Cambridge University Press
The Edinburgh Building, Cambridge CB2 8RU, UK

Published in the United States of America by
Cambridge University Press, New York

www.cambridge.org
Information on this title: www.cambridge.org/9781107629677

© Cambridge University Press 1912

First published 1912
First paperback edition 2012

A catalogue record for this publication is available from the British Library

ISBN 978-1-107-62967-7 Paperback

CONTENTS

CHAP.   PAGE

I. THE FAME OF ASSYRIA PERMEATED THE ANCIENT WORLD 1

II. ASSYRIA AS A CITY STATE 28

III. ASSYRIA'S EARLY RELATIONS WITH EGYPT, MITANNI, AND BABYLONIA 50

IV. ASSYRIA AS A WORLD POWER . . . 71

V. THE SECOND EMPIRE 83

VI. THE SARGONIDS 112

BIBLIOGRAPHY 157

INDEX 159

LIST OF ILLUSTRATIONS

Human-headed Bull Colossus . . . *Frontispiece*

FACING PAGE

An Eponym List 12

Brick of Erishum 40

Letter from Tushratta to Amenophis III. . . . 52

Statue of Ashur-Natsir-Pal I. 66

Eight-sided Prism of Tiglath-Pileser I. . . . 72

The Synchronous History 78

Black Obelisk of Shalmaneser III. . . . 94

Stele of Shamshi-Adad 100

Six-sided Prism of Sennacherib . . . 122

Heads of Enemies brought to Sennacherib . . 134

Architectural Ornaments and Bronze Repoussé Work . 150

Sennacherib superintending the transfer of a Colossus . 156

Maps of Nineveh and Assyrian Empire . . . *at end*

The illustration facing p. 156 is from Layard's *Monuments of Nineveh*, by kind permission of Messrs Chapman & Hall; the others are from photographs by Messrs Mansell & Co., those facing pp. 52 and 150 being reproduced from the *Encyclopaedia Britannica* (eleventh edition).

CHAPTER I

In the sacred Scriptures of the Hebrews we read
that "out of that land, *i.e.* Shinar or Babylonia,
went forth Asshur and builded Nineveh, and the
city Rehoboth, and Calah, and Resen between
Nineveh and Calah: the same is a great city" (Gen.
x. 11). We may be in some doubt as to the exact
meaning of these words, and before the discovery
and decipherment of the Assyrian monuments it
was permissible to conclude that "Assyria was a
great and powerful country lying on the Tigris
(Gen. ii. 14), the capital of which was Nineveh. It
derived its name apparently from Asshur the son
of Shem (Gen. x. 22), who in later times was worshipped as their chief god by the Assyrians. Asshur
may be regarded as an eponymous hero." In view
of modern knowledge as to the early history of
Assyria, different translations have been suggested
which, without doing too great violence to the

A   1

original, will bring out its real value. "Asshur was the earliest capital; Ashur its city god who became the national god of Assyria. Calah or Kalah, as we may write the name, was a later capital, and Nineveh became the capital in the time best known to the Hebrews." It is supposed that Rehoboth represents the *rêbit âli* or "broad places of the city"; Nineveh, its suburbs and extensions. Resen is not yet satisfactorily identified.

In Herodotus (I. 7) Ninus, the mythical founder of Nineveh, appears as the son of Bêlus, the mythical founder of Babylon. It is an interesting but not very profitable occupation to seek to interpret the statements of the Greek writers by comparison with the facts that may have suggested their stories. Their chief value is the eloquent testimony they bear to the lasting impression of greatness which Assyria left upon the imagination of the peoples of Asia Minor, from whom the Greeks drew their information.

It is somewhat different with the statements of Berosus, who, though he wrote in Greek, was himself a Babylonian priest, and had access to ancient and authentic sources of history. Wherever his statements admit of verification they have been found to be reliable, subject to such modifications as are usually necessary in dealing with ancient historians. Unfortunately his writings are only known to us from the extracts which Eusebius and later writers made from more ancient authorities who had quoted from him.

It would be unfair to assume that the Assyrians themselves were entirely objective and trustworthy witnesses. They, too, indulged in speculations as to their origin and early history which, while they may embody ancient traditions, in some cases founded on fact, must be treated with great reservations. They built upon identifications obviously due to the fancies of folk etymology. They glorified their ancient cities by ascribing to them a foundation in the ages before the Flood. Sargon II. refers to the 350 kings who had ruled Assyria before him. Sennacherib, in a hymn of rejoicing over a triumphal entry into Babylon, appears to deduce his descent from Gilgamesh and Engidu, mythical heroes of a prehistoric age in Babylonia. He also enumerates a list of kings who may some day be proved to have reigned in Assyria and Babylonia. Such names as Egiba, an eponymous hero of a powerful family, well known in later times as bankers and business men in Sippara, Na'id-Ashur, Ashur-gamilia, Ana-Ashur-taklaku, or Shamash-tsululushu, who may turn out to be important persons in early history, and many more are named.

It will be noted that such traditions are characteristic of a later age. Sargon or Sennacherib, who had no hereditary right to their throne, might have been glad to believe the stories of court scribes who made out for them a claim to ancient descent. They may in truth have belonged to old and honoured families, and we are not justified in dismissing these references as idle fancies. Without confirmation, however, we cannot use them for historical purposes.

The historical books of the Old Testament make a very solid contribution to the history of the relation of the peoples of Israel and Judah with Assyria. Menahem's tribute, the captivity of the Northern Israelites, the support given to Ahaz by Tiglathpileser, the capture of Damascus, Hosea's subjection to Shalmaneser, the fall of Samaria, the deportation of Israel to Halah and Habor, Sennacherib's invasion of Judæa, the siege of Jerusalem, the murder of Sennacherib by his sons, Assyria's trade with Tyre, the colonisation of Palestine under Esarhaddon, and a crowd of other references or allusions receive substantiation and elucidation from the Assyrian monuments. They also furnish important contributions to the arrangement of events, and were of inestimable value during the early stages of cuneiform decipherment.

The denunciations of Assyria by the prophets, and above all the prophecy of the fall of Nineveh by Nahum, a contemporary and perhaps eye-witness of the event, throw considerable light upon the way in which Assyria was regarded by other nations, not without eloquent parallels elsewhere. Assyria indeed laid a heavy yoke upon the nations. The Assyrians were regarded as a set of land pirates.

From the Biblical notices, even when supplemented by the other writers of antiquity, we should acquire a very limited and one-sided view of this really great nation. We could never estimate its real significance in the struggle of the nations, nor duly appreciate the influence it exerted far beyond the limits of its empire. For, in Egypt, in Tarsus, in Cappadocia and Cilicia, in Media and old Persia, in Elam and Armenia, its kings fought and conquered, imposed not only tribute but customs, left monuments and colonists whose influence extended far beyond garrison duties and threats of vengeance on rebellion. Its history has lessons even for our own day, pointedly illustrating the futility of military success without commercial and economic stability.

That history we must learn from Assyria's own monuments, not ignoring the other sources of information, but interpreting its achievements in the light of their avowed purpose and as the expression of the national character and genius.

THE NAME ASSYRIA.—The word Assyria may be regarded as a not inept rendering of Asshurai, the name given to themselves by the Assyrians. They called their land Asshur.

Asshur was originally the name of a city, which gradually dominated its neighbours and so became the nucleus of a state. How it came by that name is not easy to decide. The national god was Ashur. In later times his name is written precisely like that of the country, but earlier, A-Shur, as distinguished from the city Ash-Shur. Still earlier, his name was Ashir. We may therefore have to do with a gradual assimilation of names originally distinct.

Asshur, like most of the old states in Babylonia, had many names, all used to denote the same place, but doubtless originally pronounced differently and embodying somewhat different conceptions. A very old name was A-USAR, which may have meant "along the river bank." Another name was SHÀ-URU, possibly "the city of the heart," though it may have merely meant "metropolis." Yet another was PAL-TIL-KI, which may be "the place of the old regime." A name like URU-DUG-GA, "the good city," was possibly a term of affection, but being also the name of a southern Babylonian city, Eridu, some fancy it bears witness to an immigration from the south. It is not, however, an early name, and seems rather to be poetical in its use. However written, it is generally agreed that these names could always be read **Asshur,** than which we know of no other native name.

EARLY INHABITANTS.—A very difficult question is raised when we seek to draw conclusions as to the original inhabitants of Assyria. The names of the temples in Assyria, as well as these old names for Asshur, admit of interpretation as being Sumerian words. Now the whole culture of Assyria was founded upon that of Babylonia, where it is certain that a Semitic people took over the culture of the Sumerians, an older folk. Although these Semitic Babylonians spoke a Semitic tongue, they regarded Sumerian as a sacred language. They kept Sumerian names for gods and temples, and used Sumerian words in a modified form for many things besides those directly connected with religious rites. Now as far back as we can go the Assyrians wrote and spoke Semitic, only differing from Babylonian in dialectic forms, and they evidently derived all their literary apparatus from Babylonia. Whether they were Semites or not, with the Babylonian language, they took over the Babylonian use of Sumerian. Whether they named the temples themselves or found them already erected and named, they kept the Sumerian names in their writings. Their use of Sumerian may be compared in some respects to the use of Latin in mediæval Europe. There is, however, no proof that they did not read these

Sumerian names by their corresponding Semitic names. Hence we can argue little from this use.

NATIONAL CHARACTERISTICS.—The Assyrians differed markedly from the Babylonians in national character. They were more robust, warlike, fierce, than the mild industrial people of the south. It is doubtful whether they were much devoted to agriculture or distinguished for manufactures, arts and crafts. They were essentially a military folk. The king was a despot at home, but the general of the army abroad. The whole organisation of the state was for war. The agriculture was left to serfs or slaves. The manufactures, weaving at any rate, were done by women. The guilds of workmen were probably foreigners, as the merchants mostly were. The great temples and palaces, walls and moats, were constructed by captives. The sculptures and statues were possibly the work of native artists, as they have a style of their own, but the costlier articles of household use and the chief wealth of the people were the spoils of other nations. For the greater part of its existence Assyria was the scourge of the nations and sucked the blood of other races. It lived on the tribute of subject states, and conquest ever meant added tribute in all necessities and luxuries of life, beside an annual demand for men and horses, cattle and sheep, grain and wool to supply the needs of the army and the city. The army overshadowed everything else, and its demands and needs made incessant expeditions imperative to keep it content. Any prolonged inactivity on the part of the king endangered his throne, and while he often was able to send trusty generals to carry on distant campaigns, a victorious general was too often the next successor to the throne.

THE CITY ASSHUR.—Like the city states of Babylonia the kingdom of Assyria developed from a city, Asshur, geographically separated from them by a wide interval, but assigned, by tradition and analogy alike, an early history similar to theirs. There is, however, no record of Asshur's struggle for supremacy with neighbouring city states. In the days when Nippur, Erech, Ur and Isin became kingdoms in Babylonia, we do not know of any relations which they had with the district afterwards to become such a powerful state. It may well have been included in Súri, or Syria, and the march of the Babylonian or Sumerian conquerors to Mesopotamia probably followed the course of the Euphrates and so left Asshur aside. In those days its relations may have been rather with Elam and the north.

The earliest Semitic immigration into Babylonia, which occupied the north and reached its climax in the empire of Sargon of Akkad and his son Naram-

Sin, probably deeply affected Asshur. We can scarcely imagine that it lay outside the empire of such mighty monarchs. It was, however, a mere provincial state. When that dynasty fell the revival of the Sumerian power in the south must have left Asshur to its own development. Doubtless, the conquests of the Sumerians drove many Semites northwards, and Asshur may have received a considerable influx of fugitives from the south.

The rise to power of the Amorite dynasty in the north of Babylonia was certainly due to a large influx of Semitic folk, whose presence even in the south is monumentally attested. The dynasty of Isin included monarchs like Ishme-Dagan, whose name is the same as that of more than one ruler of Asshur. We can hardly resist the conclusion that Amorites had also invaded Asshur. The great Hammurabi, whose rule was acknowledged in Asshur and Nineveh, seems to imply that his power there had been established by force of arms, but he does not claim to have conquered the land himself.

We gain the impression that Asshur was so early flooded by Semitic immigrants that only the merest trace of non-Semitic races ever survived. When we are able to examine its own literature it appears to be simply a province of Babylonian culture.

A few outstanding facts remain to show an earlier history and a submerged race.

MITANNI.—Ushpia, Kikia, and Adasi, names of early rulers at Asshur, are neither Semitic nor Sumerian. Sargon II. gives Ishtar of Nineveh her old name of Shaushka. If this be the correct reading of the name, it recalls the offer of Tushratta, king of Mitanni, to send Ishtar of Nineveh to Egypt. This has been taken to imply that Nineveh was then subject to Mitanni, and Ishtar may have received this name as identified by Tushratta with a goddess of Mitanni. The name recalls Shaushkash, the consort of Teshup, the Mitanni weather-god. Her worship at Nineveh may have been due solely to the Mitanni conquest. At Kalah also, another Mitanni god was worshipped under the name of Ea-sharru, which may be identical with the Cilician name, Jazarmash. But the names Ushpia and Kikia at any rate are reconcilable with the assumption of an early population, akin to that of Mitanni, possibly a thousand years before the conquest of Assyria.

ELAM.—The knowledge acquired in recent times of the ancient language of Elam renders it probable that the above and many other Mitanni names are really Elamitic, and that it is to Elam we must look for the early population. Assyria's immediately northern neighbours in Nairi were possibly Elamite, while to the west and south-west Elam itself lay. How early the Semitic occupation of Elam may have taken place we do not know, nor when the Kassites first occupied the hills. They were always regarded by the Assyrians as enemies, and when they came to the throne in Babylon, Assyria was never subject to them, but held it her mission to rid Babylonia of Kassite rule. Hence the Elamite element must have been early, if present at all.

ASIRU.—A brick found at Tuzchurmati, on the Aksu, a tributary of the Adhem or Rhodanus, bears an inscription of Pukhia, son of Asiru, king of Khurshitu. It is written in Semitic. In the time of Rîm-Anum of Larsa, who conquered parts of Elam and the lands to the east of the Tigris and districts in the hills behind Assyria, there are frequent references to Bît Asiri, and a number of these Asiru people are named, bearing Semitic names. The Bît Asiri, like the Bît Adini and the Bît Iakin in Chaldea, or the Bît Amukkani, may well have been a Semitic tribe. Their date is before the First Dynasty. Some fate, of which we have no trace left, may later have driven them to seek refuge in Asshur, and they may have given their name to the country. Pukhia recalls Aushpia and Kikia in form.

CAPPADOCIA.—A number of tablets have been found in Cappadocia of the time of the Second

AN EPONYM LIST.

Dynasty of Ur which show marked affinities with Assyria. The divine name Ashir, as in early Assyrian texts, the institution of Eponyms, and many personal names which occur in Assyria, are so characteristic that we must assume kinship of peoples. But whether they witness to a settlement in Cappadocia from Assyria, or *vice versâ*, is not yet clear.

THE COUNTRY ASSHUR.—The Jebel Hamrin, a low range of hills coming north-west from the western border of Elam, crosses the Tigris below its junction with the lower Zab and runs up the west bank of the Tigris. On an outlying spur, washed on the east by the Tigris, cut off from the rest of the range on the west by a deep gorge, and presenting a steep cliff to the north over a swamp and stream, lay Asshur the first capital. It was a natural stronghold, impregnable except from the south where lay its chief fortifications over against a gravel rise from the valley below the hills. Here on Mount Abech lay the temple of Ashur with its huge temple-tower or *zikkurat*, the temple of Anu and Adad, and later many another temple, the palaces of the earlier kings, and a great city.

Across the Tigris, to the east, it became united in close bonds of union with Arbela, and beyond the upper Zab with the district, which, if it had not been the original source of Asshur's population,

was soon its chief province. Thus enlarged, the
land of Assyria may be considered as bounded by
the mountain chains of Armenia and Kurdistan
to the north and east, on the west by the Tigris,
and on the south by the Upper Zab.

This district was a natural stronghold, and con-
sisting of hilly ground, well watered in the valleys,
was fertile and populous. It contained many important cities, of which Kalah at the junction of
the Upper Zab, Nineveh on the Choser, Dûr-Sargon
to the north-east, Imgur-Bêl south-east of Nineveh,
and Tarbis to the north-west are the best known.

The climate was temperate, the slopes of the
hills well wooded with oak, plane and pine, while the
the plains produced figs, olives and vines. The
grains cultivated were wheat, barley, and millet.
In the days of its prosperity the orchards embraced
date palms, orange, lemon, pomegranate, apricot,
mulberry, and other fruit trees, more or less con-
jecturally identified. A large variety of vegetables
were grown—beans, peas, cucumbers, onions, and
lentils may be named. The hills furnished valuable building stone, the soft alabaster—on slabs of
which most of the monuments were sculptured in
low relief—fine marbles and hard limestone. Basalt
and conglomerate were worked into vessels and even
statuary. Iron, copper, and lead were obtainable
in the mountains near ; but it is not clear that the

Assyrians ever worked the mines. The lion and the wild ox were hunted, as were also the wild boar, deer, gazelle, ibex or goat, and the hare. The wild ass, mountain sheep, bear, fox, and jackal are named. The eagle was well known, and a great many birds, such as the bustard, crane, stork, wild goose, duck, partridge, plover, dove, swallow, raven, which all seem to be figured on monuments. Fish was plentiful. The Assyrians had domesticated oxen, asses, sheep, goats, and dogs. Camels and horses were introduced from abroad.

THE SOURCES OF HISTORY.—To a greater extent than is the case with most histories, that of Assyria is limited by the nature of its sources and in a manner almost unique. Beyond a few notices in classical authors and a few slight hints in the Old Testament, the history of Assyria is the product of modern research. The older notices, when reliable, are often unintelligible owing to our lack of the implied knowledge which may have made their reference clear to contemporaries.

The ancient monuments, the subject of modern research, present remarkable difficulties. Only a century ago they were still to be described as written in an unknown language and in a form of writing of which not one sign was then capable of being read. After Grotefend, in 1815, had succeeded in reading the old Persian inscriptions so far as to make out correctly the names of a few kings, and so had indicated a probable meaning for a few of the characters of the Persian cuneiform alphabet, Hincks and other scholars, such as Longperier, De Saulcy, St Martin, Rask, Lassen, Burnouf, Beer, etc., slowly, and literally letter by letter, added to the knowledge of these signs, but little could be read and less understood until our own countryman, Sir Henry Rawlinson, copied the great trilingual inscription of Darius at Behistun. He not only discovered the value of the signs, but succeeded in making an intelligible translation of the whole inscription in 1851. Later research has added but little to that work. One of the three columns was written in an entirely different form of writing, which the translation of the Old Persian column soon rendered intelligible. The language proved to be Babylonian and closely akin to Hebrew, Arabic and other languages of the Semitic group. Arguing from the meanings of similar words in the other Semitic tongues, scholars made attempts at translation, depending largely upon the newly acquired knowledge of the parallel Persian column. The knowledge so acquired was soon applied to the somewhat similar Assyrian inscriptions of which Layard had discovered large numbers. The form of writing differed considerably and the languages were not entirely the same, but Assyrian and Babylonian

are practically identical, their differences being
merely dialectical.

It is within the memory of living men that the
reading of Biblical names like Sargon, Sennacherib,
Jehu, Omri or Ahab on the Assyrian monuments
excited the greatest wonder and interest. Each
name so read was a fresh triumph of the most
laborious research, experiment, and scholarly
intuition. The chapter of research is not entirely
closed, for apart from the fact that only a fraction
of the total number of Assyrian inscriptions, hoarded
in the British Museum and elsewhere, has yet been
published, the explorers of the ancient East are
almost daily bringing fresh material to light. In
consequence of this perpetually growing mass of
material the attempts made to write a History of
Assyria are still doomed to be incomplete. Any
day may bring more information to be embodied.

It is therefore a triumph of the most remarkable
research ever yet made in the way of decipherment
that one is able to write a history of Assyria at all.
The nature of that research has imposed certain
restrictions. The country had its earliest capital
at the city of Asshur, then the seat of government
was transferred to Kalah, lastly to Nineveh. Now
it was at Kalah that Layard first excavated his
finest monuments; then he and his successors
recovered from Nineveh the overwhelming majority

B

of all the Assyrian monuments that have come to
Europe. Somewhat earlier Botta had obtained a
large amount of material from Dûr-Sargon. Very
little came from the old capital, Asshur. Since
1903, however, the *Deutsche Orientgesellschaft* have
been exploring Asshur. They have nearly doubled
the number of monarchs of Assyria known to us,
but it will be many years before the new material
is published. The brief notices which the explorers on the spot send home appear regularly in
the *Mitteilungen*, only serving to make all scholars
long for more detailed information. One may feel
sure that a German scholar would not willingly
leave much for future students to discover or
correct, but the monuments have lain so long buried
that they are often encrusted with earthy salts.
To remove these without damaging stone, often itself
nearly rotten, may appear almost hopeless, yet it
is usually done with success. Till it has been done
much remains unread.

The greatest difficulty of all is that the monuments are so often fragmentary that it happens,
with a frequency almost comical, that just at the
moment when the narrative grows interesting, an
unfortunate break in the stone or lacuna in the
document destroys all hope of recovering the
original record. Against this may be set the
fortunate circumstance that the Assyrian monarchs,

as if foreseeing the perishable nature of their records, caused them to be multiplied to such an extent that there is always reasonable hope of discovering a duplicate. Further, many kings take special pleasure in repeating the information given on the monuments of their predecessors.

As a result of all these hindrances to complete and exhaustive treatment, the history, so far as it can be reconstructed, is singularly disconnected. Although we can no longer have much doubt as to its general course, some of the most important events have but slight records, while by some accident of preservation or discovery far less valuable records are full to the minutest detail. We are obliged for the time to take the view of one writer, and that the most interested of all. We may well hesitate to take without demur all that a king says for himself, but we have no option. There is no other side to the question. Scepticism may easily be pushed too far, and in any case there is no alternative to suggest. The result is a patchwork of contemporary but uncritical material which can only be considered provisionally attested. It will be well to point out where doubt is legitimate and where future discovery may well be expected to bring about revision or extension.

It is very unlikely that either the name of a king or the length of his reign would be invented or falsified. Nor would the conquest of a country which never existed be ascribed to him. When a king claims to have conquered a certain land he may only have succeeded in imposing his authority, exacting tribute and military service. It is practically certain that the conquered land would rebel at the first opportunity. Permanent conquest could only be expected after decimating the population, or transporting them wholesale to a district where they would be dependent on the king's power. The struggle for existence was so keen that Assyria must go under unless she broke for ever the power of her neighbours. She did that, but ultimately exhausted herself by undertaking to rule a wider empire than she could manage. We can hardly expect her to have seen where to stop, and her history, up to the eve of her fall, was a long pæan of victory, broken only by the silence which covers temporary reverses. For the twentieth time the Assyrian conquered " all lands," called himself monarch " of all points of the compass," but though he truly " trod down all the unsubmitting," the next king went cheerfully out to do it all again. Vigorous reprisals, joyous victory, cleansing fires of adversity, made up the glorious warrior's life, produced a people hard to beat. Ultimately they spread out too thin over too large an area, and could not rally in sufficient force to protect the heart of the empire. So they went under, but it was a gay time while it lasted. A certain boldness of outlook made careful, cautious statement a fault in style; while each king hated to seem less successful than his predecessors.

It is very difficult to prove that any Assyrian inscription is deliberately false, but it would be absurd to take every statement as literally true because made on the monuments and engraven in stone, or because it was written in cuneiform and stored in the library of an ancient Assyrian temple or palace. We are continually told of the large numbers of the enemy who met the king in battle, or the thouands of captives he took, and we may well treat these numbers as signs of boastful exaggeration. We cannot credit that the small states of Mesopotamia could furnish time after time such populations as alone could justify the figures given. Nor can we credit the amount of spoil stated to have been carried to Asshur. The city could not have held it, nor could the despoiled lands have furnished it again so soon. But when the king narrates his journey from city to city we cannot suppose that the cities he names are imaginary in position or number. Though lately burnt down by his predecessors, the scattered people would soon gather to the old home. The indications afforded by these inscriptions are thus invaluable for ancient historical geography and usually reliable, but we may suspect some of them of recording as separate cities different names of the same place.

The later kings of Assyria delighted to record scraps of information about their predecessors, which are often the only source we have for early history. These may in some cases be due to tradition, and have therefore been treated by many scholars with natural reserve. When, however, a king is relating the restoration of an ancient building, he probably, in the process of clearing the foundations for his new work, had access to ancient records. For the builders usually inscribed their name and titles, along with their genealogy, upon bricks, pavement tiles, wall decorations, and in the foundation deposits of cylinders, prisms, and votive offerings.

From such records found *in situ* we can still identify, not only city sites, but the temples, palaces, gates, walls and other buildings with absolute certainty. There could be little temptation to falsify such information. The later monarch may, however, have been misled as to the date of his predecessor, and such dates require careful treatment. Scribes may have wished to please their king by exaggerating the antiquity of their city's history, but the names they preserve are probably reliable.

(a) Thus when Shalmaneser I. restored the temple of Ashur, " the dwelling of the gods, the house of Ashur," he left four stone tablets inscribed with the same inscription, naming himself as son of Adad-nirari, grandson of Arik-dên-ili. He ascribes the founding of the temple to Aushpia. This temple, he says, was restored by Erishum, priest of Ashur, and after 159 years it was again restored by Shamshi-Adad, the priest of Ashur. It was destroyed by fire early in Shalmaneser's own reign, 580 years later, as he states. As we know on other grounds that Shalmaneser I. lived about B.C. 1320, we must thus put Shamshi-Adad about 1900 B.C., and Erishum about 2060 B.C. Aushpia must be placed still earlier.

Now Esarhaddon also restored this temple, and his account seems different in some respects. He also names Aushpia as the founder. Then he names Irishum, son of Ilushumma, as its restorer. Then after 126 years the temple fell, and Shamshi-Adad, son of Bêlkabi, rebuilt it. Again, after 434 years, it was burnt down, and Shalmaneser I. rebuilt it. Here he seems to put about 180 years less than Shalmaneser does between Erishum and that king. It is clear that he has made no mistake as to the names of the builders. It is usual to suppose that Shalmaneser, being at least 600 years earlier in date, would have better information. But it is quite possible that Esarhaddon did not ascribe the various restorations to the same persons. We are not yet in a position to correct or harmonise these conflicting statements.

(b) Tiglath-Pileser I., who calls himself son of Ashur-resh-ishi and grandson of Mutakkil-Nusku, rebuilt another temple in Asshur, that of Anu and Adad. He states that it had once been built by Shamshi-Adad, son of Ishme-Dagan, and after 641 years it fell into ruins and was taken down by Ashur-dân with a view to restoration, but lay unrestored till Tiglath-Pileser's time. As Ashur-dân was his great grandfather we may allow an interval of 60 years and so put this Shamshi-Adad 700 years before Tiglath-Pileser, who reigned about 1120 B.C. We may therefore place him about B.C. 1820.

We are thus confirmed in our presumption that Shalmaneser's names are correct and his dates probable. Esarhaddon gives additional information as to the parentage of the restorer whom he names.

It will be noted that such references as the ascription of a certain event to a certain king, without statement of the year of his reign, leave us a wide margin for dates. We do not know from what year in his own reign the king counts, nor up to what year of the reign he quotes.

(c) Sennacherib has left a record that, after his

conquest of Babylon, therefore soon after 689 B.C., he brought back to Assyria a jewel which Tukulti-Ninip 600 years before had captured from the treasures of Shagaraktishuriash, a Kassite king of Babylon. Now we know that a Shagaraktishuriash king of Babylon was father of Kashtiliash II., king of Babylon, whom Tukulti-Ninip I. carried away captive to Assyria. Therefore we may place Tukulti-Ninip I. about 1290 B.C.

(d) Again Sennacherib, in his inscription on the rocks at Bavian, a village north of Mosul, whence he had brought water supplies for his great city of Nineveh, tells us that after 418 years he brought back from Babylon to the city of Ekallâte its gods Adad and Shala which had been carried away from thence by Marduk-nâdin-akhê in the time of Tiglath-Pileser. Now we know that Tiglath-Pileser I. was a contemporary of Marduk-nâdin-akhê, and are thus able to date his reign about 1107 B.C.

It will have been noticed that Shalmaneser I. and Tiglath-Pileser I., in Statements (a) and (b), give their own genealogy, naming their fathers and grandfathers. This was the usual practice with all the Assyrian rulers. Consequently we are able to trace the lineal descent of the throne from father to son for many generations. Indeed there is great probability that one and the same family ruled for over 700 years.

The kings frequently name earlier rulers as their predecessors on the throne of Assyria. These statements serve as valuable checks upon other statements, and one result has been to establish the fact that an Assyrian king often calls a predecessor *abî*, literally " my father," when he merely means to record his lineal descent, it may be, from a very distant forefather.

A very few more inscriptions would set the series of kings, from Ilushumma down to the fall of Nineveh, in its correct order without a blank. A somewhat frequent recurrence of the same name has hitherto led to some confusion, but the recent discoveries at Asshur have filled up an almost hopeless series of gaps and introduced order into something like chaos. We can hardly expect that many more rulers are yet to be discovered for the last two thousand years of Assyrian history.

Of great use in the arrangement of the kings in their proper order are the synchronisms between them and foreign rulers, particularly those of Babylonia. In this the Babylonian *Synchronous History* is a document of the first importance. It records the successive rectifications of boundaries between Assyria and Babylonia, giving the kings concerned in them from about B.C. 1600 to B.C. 800. Copies were preserved in the Library of Ashur-bânipal at Nineveh, and are now in the British Museum.

The Assyrian *Eponym Canon* gave a list of these officers, who, like the Archons at Athens or the Consuls at Rome, gave a name to the year. We possess lists of this kind, which commence in B.C. 911 and extended to B.C. 640. The accession of a new king was always recorded; and the mention in one place of the solar eclipse of June 15th B.C. 763 fixes the series of dates accurately for the whole period. Several copies are now in the British Museum. The *Canon of Ptolemy*, beginning with B.C. 747, overlaps this and gives welcome if unnecessary confirmation.

The Egyptian chronology gives valuable assistance for the period of the fifteenth and fourteenth centuries B.C. The synchronisms with the Hittite, Mitanni and Elamite kings are already of value, and more may be expected from these sources as the information with respect to these long-forgotten empires is enlarged by exploration and excavation in the East.

CHAPTER II

IT is at present impossible to determine at what date Asshur absorbed its neighbour cities and extended its dominion over Arbela and Nineveh. Indeed, that may not have been the true story of its expansion. There are some indications that Asshur and its neighbouring states entered into a sort of confederacy, perhaps under the pressure of a common foe. Asshur was for early methods of warfare a natural stronghold and a splendid city of refuge. Every indication points to the fact that its population was perpetually reinforced by fugitives from Babylonia. As in the case of the Babylonian cities its *patesis*, or city governors, on one side high priests of the city god Ashur and his earthly representatives; on the other, mayors of the town, would soon lay claim to the title of king.

A king, according to the conception of his powers which we find prevailing in Assyria, had a right to expect military support from his subject cities. He had a principal share of the lands and spoil of conquered peoples, and as protector of the temples

was entitled to borrow from their treasures.   He had
also land and estates as endowment of his office.
But he was not able to appropriate the property
of his subjects at will.   Military service was com-
pulsory on all adult males, but only for a limited
number of calls.   These citizen soldiers were a militia,
the *ummanâti* of the inscriptions, and as time went
on they were increasingly relieved by bodies of
regular troops whose exact functions are not clearly
to be distinguished.   The *kurâdi* "heroes" or
veterans and the *kitsir sharrâti*, or "King's Own
Regiments," appear to be regulars and used on all
distant expeditions.   The militia could not be long
taken away from agricultural duties, and were
ultimately only called out on occasions of great
urgency.   The soldiers were paid by booty or
prize money.

The king apparently furnished weapons, but the
owners of estates upon whom it was incumbent
to furnish one or more men for the militia found
also clothing and rations for the campaign.   A
subject city was in the position of a corporate
estate owner and had its fixed quota of men to
furnish, for whom it was responsible.

Each city had its own laws, and levied its own
rates and taxes.   Conquered cities paid tribute in
men and money.   But municipal independence was
the rule.   The men of Asshur paid dues in Nineveh

exactly as if they were foreigners, and that long after Assyria became an empire. Latterly it became a custom for the king to exempt by a rescript certain persons from various dues, and confer privileges of free entrance to and exit from certain areas. This was usually done as a reward for personal service to the king or state.

The subject cities were very jealous of their civic rights and customs. It was the secret of popularity for a king to conserve them. When the population had become large enough these rights included freedom from the *corvée* or forced labour on public works. Tiglathpileser IV. was regarded as an oppressor of the old cities because he demanded from their citizens such indignities, and it was the proud boast of Sargon II. that he had freed them from such oppression.

The construction of the Eponym lists indicates that the cities of Assyria formed a confederacy. There was a regular rota of officials who gave their name in turn to the years of a reign. It began with the king himself, and when the court had developed he was followed by the Tartan or Commander-in-chief of the Forces, the Grand Chamberlain, the Chief Cup-bearer and the Chief Baker, Chief Justice, etc., offices often conferred on successful generals. Next, at all times, followed the governors or viceroys of the old cities. These were Asshur, often simply

called "the land," Nineveh, Arbela and Kalah.
As the kingdom grew other cities or provinces
were included. Thus latterly Carchemish, Samaria,
even distant Kummukh or Commagene, furnished
Eponyms. The Eponym for the year was originally
chosen by lot, a practice which nominally continued to
the last. But the lot fell with convenient appropriate-
ness upon the governors of the right places, as a rule.
The year in which the governor was chosen Eponym
was called the *limmu* of that governor, and documents were dated in that year as falling in his
limmu. The Eponyms, like Archons at Athens
or Consuls at Rome, thus gave their name to the
year. There is, however, no trace of any other
special power which the *limmu* conferred. The
Eponym had no special duties to perform, but there
is no doubt that his honour commemorated a time
when the Eponym was chief of the entire state.
His appointment was made in the closing days of the
year, and he entered office on the first of Nisan.
When the king died the new king started the rota
afresh. But it is significant of the importance
once attached to the position that after his Eponymy
the rota was often carried out as if the accession
had caused no break. The states could hardly have
clung so pertinaciously to a mere naming of the year
if it had not been the last shred of a once acknowledged right to temporary supremacy.

For some time we can only speak of the *patesis* of Asshur, though they may often have claimed the title of king. We may regard the first period as one in which the city Asshur was gradually gaining supremacy at home. How soon it took precedence in Assyria proper, or included Arbela or Nineveh in its confederation, we do not know. We have no record of wars with either.

THE EARLIEST RULERS OF ASSHUR.—Some of the earliest references to the rulers of Asshur designate them as *patesi*. In the case of the old Babylonian city states it has been noticed that when a state like Lagash came under the supremacy of the kings of Ur, its own rulers, even the powerful Gudea, whose public works were such as any king might be proud to have erected, make no claim to the title of king, but content themselves with that of *patesi*. Hence it has been thought that the title *patesi* denoted an inferior status and that its holder implicitly renounced all claim to be an independent monarch. When, therefore, the later kings of Assyria recorded the names of earlier rulers and gave them the title of *patesi*, in view of the evident dependence of Assyria upon Babylonia in all matters of culture, religion and political organisation, it seemed legitimate to assume that the same implications held for the use of the title in Assyria.

The designation of an Assyrian ruler as a *patesi*

of Ashur has very commonly been taken to imply
an admission of dependence upon a higher power,
and Babylonia was naturally supposed to be the
higher power in question. This view cannot be
pressed. The sovereign to whom the *patesi* was
subordinate was divine. The *patesi* claimed to be
the viceroy on earth of his god ; and that he still
was, within the limit of his own domains. His
subjection to an earthly sovereign might or might
not invalidate his claim to be a king, but did not
affect his relation to his city god.

When Asshur was independent its kings continued
to call themselves *patesi* of Ashur. In cases where
their inscription was concerned with internal politics
alone, especially in the erection of temples, walls,
wells, canals, etc., a king might be content to speak
of himself as *patesi*. In inscriptions recording his
conquests he would claim to be a king. We cannot, therefore, press the meaning of *patesi* to imply
subjection to an overlord. Nor, on the other hand,
is it possible to argue independence from the use of
the title king. Many overlords took to themselves
the title " king of kings " and allowed their vassals
still to be called kings.

The term *patesi* may really be a Sumerian word
borrowed by the Semitic Babylonians along with
the office. They, however, especially in Assyria,
rendered it, and perhaps read it, in Semitic by

c

ishshakku. That may mean little more than "headman," a parallel to the Arab sheik. The Sumerian *patesi*, however, seems to have denoted a "steward," and many owners of large estates had their own *patesi*. The *patesi* of Ashur was "the High Steward" of the god, but it soon became a pure title. The *patesi* was probably the hereditary Headman of the clan, which claimed to be the aristocracy of the town. He was as such the titular High priest of the city-god. It is, however, scarcely accurate to render the term either as priest or king or even priest-king. The Assyrian rulers were also priests, and when they chose to emphasise the fact they called themselves *Shangû*, which means " priest " simply.

The combination of varied offices in one person can never be a justification for the identification of the offices. When, then, we record of a certain ruler that he is entitled *patesi*, priest or king, we must not assume that he was anything else than what the title states ; nor can we argue that he was not more.

We frequently find that a ruler is called the *shaknu* of a god, or of a state. The term means solely a *locum tenens*. The *shaknu* of a city was the *viceroy* of its king. When a king styles himself *Shaknu* of Bêl he claims to be viceregent of that god upon earth. That he was governor of the city

or country was also true, but is not the im-
plication of the term so much as its political
consequence.

We may now record what is known of each of
these early rulers.

AUSHPIA.—In an inscription of Shalmaneser I.
(see p. 23) recording his restoration of the temple
of Ashur, burnt down at the beginning of his reign,
we are told that it had been built or restored by a
series of rulers, at the head of whom was to be
placed Aushpia. Esarhaddon also enumerates
the monarchs who built at the same temple. His
list has important variations, but it places Aushpia
first. He preceded Ilushuma, who was contemporary with the founder of the First Dynasty of
Babylon. The name seems to be Elamite, or perhaps
Mitanni. We have no means of assigning an ap-
proximate date to this ruler.

KIKIA.—In an inscription of Ashur-rîm-nishêshu,
Kikia is placed first in a list of Assyrian monarchs
who built the city wall of Asshur. It is, of course,
impossible to say whether the city began with a
temple of Ashur or whether its wall was built first.
The name does not seem to be Semitic and may
be Elamite or Mitanni. We cannot date this ruler
with any certainty.

ADASI AND BÊLBANI.—In his inscription, on the
stele set up at Sendjirli, in North Syria, on which

he commemorates his conquest of Tirhakah of Ethiopia and Ba'al of Tyre, Esarhaddon declares that he was " of the seed royal, remote descendant of Bêl-bani, son of Adasi, who established the kingship of Asshur, who at the command of Adad, Shamash, Nabû and the other great gods smote off the yoke." As Sargon, his grandfather, and his father, Sennacherib, so far as we yet know, did not make this claim, possibly Esarhaddon claimed through his mother, who is thought by some to have been a Babylonian princess.

In an inscription, commemorating his buildings in Assyria and Babylonia, he calls himself " distant descendant of Bêl-bani, king of Assyria, whom long ago the decree of Marduk called to rule the land and raised their *patesi*-hood to a kingdom." If these words be correctly understood, Esarhaddon means that Bêl-bani first made Assyria a kingdom. Its former rulers had been only *patesis*, as we know many of them were. That Marduk, city god of Babylon, decreed the change may be taken to imply that previously they were subject to Babylon. In his devotion to the city, for which he had done so much, Esarhaddon may be asserting Babylonian claims beyond the exact state of the case, but many indications go to substantiate the claim.

In another inscription, dedicated to Nanâ of Erech, Esarhaddon claims to be " the offspring of Asshur,

descendant of Bêl-bani, son of Adasi, king of Asshur."
If we rightly understand Esarhaddon, Adasi must
be put at the very beginning, at least of the Semitic
occupation of Asshur. We have, however, no indication of his date.

BÊL-KAPKAPU I.—Adad-nirari IV., on his stone
tablet from Kalah, asserts that he was "the remote
descendant of Bêl-kapkapi, a king who went before
him, before the rule of Sulili." In view of the spell-
ings of Sumu-abu's name as Su-abu, and of Sumu-
la-ilu's name as Sumu-li-el, Sumu-lili, etc., it is
very likely that Sulili is intended for Sumu-la-ilu,
who is thus reckoned as a king of Assyria. We
know that Hammurabi, fifth in descent from him,
did rule Assyria and there is nothing against the
assumption that Sumu-la-ilu did also. Bêl-kapkapu
would thus be not far removed in time from Ilushumma, who fought with Sumu-abu. Whatever
the issue of that conflict, Bêl-kapkapu cannot be
placed before Sumu-la-ilu and also after Ilushumma,
for the latter's family form an unbroken line from
father to son for five generations. Bêl-kapkapu
must therefore be earlier than Sumu-abu himself.
The reason may be that while Sumu-abu was un-
successful against Ilushumma, Sumu-la-ilu may
have established a real supremacy over Assyria,
which lasted till Hammurabi's time. On the other
hand, Sulili may have nothing to do with Sumula-ilu,

but be one of the early non-Semitic rulers, like
Aushpia, Kikia and Adasi. The form of the name
suggests the iteration so characteristic of Elamite
names, and in any case was not Assyrian.

We may note that our Bêl-kapkapu has been
thought by some to be identical with Bêl-kabi, below.

IGUR-KAP-KAPU.—A brick from Asshur contains
the inscription of one Samsi-Adad, *patesi* of Ashur,
son of Igur-kap-kapu, builder of the temple of
Ashur. The similarity of this name, and the sug-
gestion that the iteration in *kapkapu* may point to
an Elamite source, have led to their identification.
Then *Igur* might in some way be another name,
Elamite or Mitanni, for Bêl. Another inscription,
on a circular piece of onyx or agate, names Shamshi-
Adad as builder of the temple of Ashur. In
spite of the difference in spelling, this may be the
same person as Samsi-Adad. Now Shalmaneser I.
records that a Shamshi-Adad, whom Esarhaddon
apparently makes son of Bêl-kabi, built at the
temple of Ashur. Some would then identify all
the three Shamshi-Adads who built at the temple
of Ashur, and therefore make Igur-kap-kapu the
same as Bêl-kabi. This would support the view
that Igur-kap-kapu was also the same as the above
Bêl-kapkapu. But then his son, Shamshi-Adad,
who could at latest be contemporary with Sumu-
abu in order to be before Sumu-la-ilu, must have

closely preceded Ilushumma. But **Shalmaneser I.** puts him 159 years later than Ilushumma's **son** Erishum, and Esarhaddon at least 126 years. As we know the series of rulers from Ilushumma for five generations, we then must bring down Sulili a century, when Adadnirari would surely have known of many earlier kings to name. Hence it is unlikely that the Shamshi-Adad who built at Asshur and was son of Bêl-kabi can have been as early as Sulili. Hence Bêl-kabi cannot be the same as Bêl-kapkapu. We can hardly identify Igur-kapkapu then with either of these. So we must leave him as the father of Samsi-Adad and put him by himself for the present. The characters of his inscription point to an early date.

SHAMSHI-ADAD I. is the same as Samsi-Adad above named as son of Igur-kap-kapu. The more usual spelling is Shamshi-Adad. Samsi-Adad recalls the names of Samsu-iluna and Samsu-ditana, kings of the First Dynasty of Babylon. If any significance is to be attached to this form it might be taken as pointing to a West Semitic or Amorite origin. But it is sufficient to note his claim to be very early on account of the style of his inscription.

BÂSHA-ASHIR.—In an inscription found at Asshur, Ashur-rîm-nishêshu relates that he rebuilt the city wall of Asshur which Kikia, Sharru-kîn, **Bâsha-Ashir** and Ashir-nirari had built.

We learn from an inscription set up by a certain
Bàsha-Ashir, *patesi* of Ashur, son of Ashir-nirari,
patesi of Ashur, that he rebuilt a temple of Ishtar
of Assyria at Asshur, which Ilushumma, a former
prince, had built and which Sharrukîn, "my father,"
(*i.e.* ancestor) had restored. We therefore conclude
that there were two rulers of the name Bàsha-
Ashir, one who restored the city wall *after* Sharrukîn
and *before* Ashir-nirari, another who built the Ishtar
temple *after* Ashir-nirari, whose son he was.

Further, we know that Ilushumma was son of
Shalim-akhum and grandson of a Bàsha-Ashir.
We therefore have the series, Bàshi-Ashir I., his
son Shalim-akhum, his son Ilushumma, his son
Erishum, his son Ikunum, his son Sharrûkin, and
then follow Ashir-nirari and his son Bàsha-Ashir
II. As the last named calls Sharrukîn his ancestor
we may assume that the whole series was one
of unbroken lineal descent from Bàsha-Ashir I. to
Bàsha-Ashir II.

SHALIM-AKHUM.—We only know of this ruler
that he was a *patesi* of Ashur, and son of Bàsha-
Ashir I.

ILUSHUMMA.—We know that one Ilushumma
fought with Sumu-abum, the founder of the First
Dynasty of Babylon. We do not, however, know
the upshot of the struggle, but as the mention of
this synchronism occurs in a chronicle of the achieve-

BRICK OF ERISHUM.

ments of Babylonian kings, and they would be unlikely to record reverses, we may assume that Assyria was beaten. Adadnirari IV. seems to imply that Sumu-la-ilu once was overlord of Assyria, and Hammurabi certainly was. Ilushumma was son of Shalim-akhum. He built a temple of Ishtar, at Asshur, and was succeeded by his son Erishum.

ERISHUM.—Erishum, or Irishum, as his name is also spelt, was son of Ilushumma. He was *patesi* of Ashur, and constructed a canal close to the great *zikkurat* or temple stage tower in Asshur. He was one of the early temple builders at Asshur, rebuilding the temple of Ashur built by Aushpia, and a temple of Adad. He lived 159 years before Shamshi-Adad III., according to Shalmeneser I., and 126 years before Shamshi-Adad II., according to Esarhaddon. He was succeeded by his son Ikunum.

IKUNUM.—Ikunum was the son of Erishum. He rebuilt the city wall of Asshur, which doubtless had been injured in the time of his grandfather's war with Babylon. He also built a temple of Ninkigal, probably in Nineveh. He was succeeded by his son Sharrûkîn I.

SHARRÛKÎN I.—This ruler bore the name afterwards to be so famous as that of Sargon II. It had already been borne by the celebrated Sargon of Akkad, if not by other Babylonian kings as well.

He rebuilt the temple of Ishtar, probably at Asshur.

BÊL-DABI or BÊL-KABI.—The name of this king or *patesi* is mentioned in the oath taken by parties to a business contract in the first year of Sinmuballit, in Sippar. The oath is " by Sinmuballit, Bêl-dabi (?) and his wife." Now, comparing the cases of Shamshi-Adad II. and Hammurabi, or of Sumu-la-ilu and other vassal kings of Sippara, we are justified in assuming that Bêl-dabi was a vassal of Sinmuballit's. It has been conjectured that, like Shamshi-Adad II., he may have been an Assyrian king or *patesi*. The name Bêl-dabi has no parallel among the known names of Assyrian rulers. But the document itself renders this reading very unlikely. It may well be Bêl-kapkabi or Bél-kabi. We have seen that Bêl-kapkapu I. was a very early ruler, and this would be Bêl-kapkapu II., but if he be Bêl-kabi and the father of the Shamshi-Adad, who was contemporary with Hammurabi, this would agree well with Esarhaddon's inscription.

The mention of this ruler's wife is exceptional. We have to go down to the days of Sammuramat (Semiramis ?) wife of Adadnirari IV. to find a parallel. She was probably a Babylonian princess. May not this be the explanation here also ? If Bêl-kabi married a daughter of a king of Babylon, and attended with her to honour the first year of

Sinmuballit, it would be natural, especially if she were the latter's sister, for a Babylonian scribe to honour them both in this way. Naturally, until we know more of the history of the period we can only indulge in conjecture. It would, however, explain the next king Hammurabi's care for the well-being of Assyria. He returned to Asshur its protecting deity, evidently carried off to Babylon, perhaps by Sumuabu.

If the above suggestions turn out to be well founded we may read this ruler's name Bêl-kabi.

SHAMSHI-ADAD II.—We have seen reason to place next the contemporary of Hammurabi, and to suppose him the son of the last named ruler. If we accept Shalmaneser's figures we must place the restorer of the Asshur wall, to whom he refers, 580 years before his own time, and that would be about 1900 B.C. Now if Erishum be really 159 years earlier we should date him about 2060 B.C. On the usually accepted chronology of the First Dynasty of Babylon we may put Erishum about 2030 B.C. The tendency of late years has been to reduce this date, but obviously it cannot be further reduced without violence to Shalmaneser's statements. If we take Erishum as about 2030 B.C. and Esarhaddon's Shamshi-Adad on his figures as 126 years later, we have a date 1900 B.C. for Shamshi-Adad as on Shalmaneser's figures. It is tempting to suppose that Shalmaneser I. and Esarhaddon intend the same Shamshi-Adad. The one king may reckon from the beginning, the other from the end, of Erishum's reign.

KIKI-BÊL.—If this be really the name of the father of the Shamshi-Adad who restored the temple of Ninkigal at Nineveh, which had been built by Ikunum, son of Erishum, we cannot place him earlier and he may be much later. Kiki-Bêl may not have been a ruler of Assyria, though his son was.

SHAMSHI-ADAD III.—The son of Kiki-Bèl, probably, rebuilt the temple of the Ninkigal, at Nineveh apparently. We are unable to place him earlier, and he may have to exchange places with some of the later rulers of the same name. He can hardly be identified with either Shamshi-Adad I. or II. If we place him here we avoid clashing with Shamshi-Adad IV.

Shalmaneser I. speaks of a certain Shamshi-Adad who built the temple of Ishtar at Nineveh, which fell in the great earthquake that also seems to have destroyed the temple of Ashur at Asshur, early in his reign. It is just possible that Ninkigal is the same as Ishtar, and that this Shamshi-Adad was the above son of Kiki-Bêl. He may, of course, be either Shamshi-Adad I. or II.

ISHME-DAGAN I.—Tiglath-pileser I. states that Shamshi-Adad, *patesi* of Ashur, son of Ishme-Dagan, built a temple of Anu and Adad in Asshur. This temple was taken down by Ashurdân, Tiglath-pileser's great grandfather, with a view to rebuilding it. This occurred about 60 years before Tiglath-pileser's time, and according to him 641 years after Shamshi-Adad, who may therefore be put about 1815 B.C. This Shamshi-Adad is thus too late to have been a contemporary of Hammurabi's, and cannot be identified with either of the Shamshi-Adads named before. He rebuilt the temple of Ashur in Asshur. We also know of an Ishme-Dagan who was father of Ashur-nirari I., who may be dated about 1700 B.C. Hence we denote this ruler as Ishme-Dagan I.

SHAMSHI-ADAD IV.—Son of Ishme-Dagan I., built the temple of Anu and Adad in Asshur about B.C. 1815, as above.

ISHME-DAGAN II.—Only known as father of the next ruler.

ASHIR-NIRARI I.—He was a restorer of the great city wall, and built the temple of Bêl shiprîa in Asshur. He was *patesi* of Ashur, and son of Ishme-Dagan II.

BÀSHA-ASHIR II.—We have already seen that he was son of Ashir-nirari I., *patèsi* of Ashur, and rebuilt the *Bît shukhuri* of Ishtar of Asshur.

OTHER RULERS CALLED SHAMSHI-ADAD.—We have already distinguished, and with more or less pro-

bability placed four rulers called Shamshi-Adad.
The list is by no means exhausted. Later we shall
be able to place more bearers of the name, but
there are others whom we cannot yet fix.

A. We have an inscription of a very important
Shamshi-Adad who calls himself *shar kishshati*, a
term which may be rendered "king of the universe" or "king of hosts," and is usually taken to
imply possession of Haran. He was a builder of
the temple of Asshur. He spells Asshur in the same
way as does the Samsi-Adad who was son of
Igur-kap-kapu. This may well be an archaism of no
great significance. We can hardly identify him with
Shamshi-Adad I., because he is not only a king
himself, but says " Anu and Bêl had selected him
from all the kings who went before him to do great
acts." Further, he speaks of a king who preceded
him, unfortunately without giving his name. He
also built the temple of Bêl in Asshur, called *E-am-
kurkurra*. He may be credited possibly with
introducing the worship of Bêl into Assyria. He
further boasts of having brought into Asshur the
spoils of the kings of Tukrish and of the kings of
the upper lands. He set up a stele with the story
of his achievements in the land of Labân, on the
border of the Great Sea ; by which we may perhaps
understand Lebanon by the Mediterannean. He
claims that there was such plenty in his day that a

shekel of silver would buy two cor of grain, about double the usual quantity, or fifteen minas of wool, or twenty measures of oil. Clearly a notable monarch ! All the more may we regret that he did not name his father nor give any indication of his own period.

B. On a circular plate of onyx or agate, now in the British Museum, we read of a Shamshi-Adad who built at the temple of Ashur. He also spells Asshur as do Shamshi-Adad I., and No. A above, but this is not sufficient to warrant any identification.

The next three rulers are inseparable, but their position is very uncertain.

ASHIR-RABI I. is mentioned by his grandson, Ashur-rîm-nishêshu, as father of Ashir-nirari II. and *patesi* of Ashur. He is generally identified with the king Ashur-irbi, who set up his image and stele at Mount Atalur, in North Syria.

ASHIR-NIRARI II. son of the last named, was also *patesi* of Ashur, and is mentioned by his son, Ashir-rîm-nîshêshu.

ASHIR-RÎM-NÎSHÊSHU, son of the last named, *patesi* of Ashur, rebuilt the wall of his city, Asshur.

We are now able to avail ourselves of the *Synchronous History* and so emerge from a very obscure period into comparatively historical times. The *Synchronous History*, as it is usually called, was drawn up with the purpose of recording the mutual relations of Assyria and Babylonia. It covered the period from 1450 B.C. to 700 B.C. It seems to have been compiled in the reign of Adad-nirari IV. The existing copies, now in the British Museum, were made for Ashurbanipal's Library at Nineveh. The commencement is, unfortunately, lost, but the first entry preserved states that Kara-indash, king of Karduniash, the name of Babylonia under the Kassite kings, and Ashur-bêl-nishêshu, king of Asshur, mutually agreed to a compact and swore to observe the boundary as settled between them. In the next entry we find that Puzur-Ashur, king of Asshur, and Burnaburiash, king of Karduniash, did the same.

We may at once note that Assyria is already a kingdom and has made good its claim to treat on terms of equality with Babylonia. Further, we have two synchronisms with Babylonian monarchs, which help greatly to fix events.

Now Adad-nirari I. states that a certain Puzur-Ashur built the wall of the new quarter of Asshur, thus enclosing a large area which lay to the south of the old city, and taking in the whole hill on which the city stood. He also built a sort of wing which cut off access to the shore below the city walls, on the Tigris, and so gave protection to the quay. The wall of the new city was further strengthened by an Ashur-bâl-nishêshu, and again, when it had fallen, was rebuilt by Erba-Adad, who was the father of Adad-nirari's great grandfather.

We must then allow for either two kings called Puzur-Ashur, or two called Ashur-bêl-nishêshu, or two of each name.

Puzur-Ashur I. built the wall of the new city and the wall protecting the quay on the Tigris. His name is written with the older spelling, Ashir.

Ashur-bêl-nishêshu I. repaired or strengthened the wall of the new city. If this was a work continuing and completing the work of Puzur-Ashur I., we may have to consider this king as the son or immediate successor of Puzur-Ashur I. In that case there must be two of the name, one here and one before Puzur-Ashur II. Some scholars would identify him with Ashur-rîm-nishêshu, and so bring in here the series, Ashir-rabi I., Ashir-nirari I., between him and Puzur-Ashur I. In that case the work which he completed was protracted over four reigns.

Later we must return to Puzur-Ashur II. and Ashur-bêl-nishêshu II. First, however, we must consider the light thrown on Assyrian history by two external sources, the Tell-el-Amarna tablets and the Egyptian inscriptions on the one hand, and the discoveries at Boghaz-koï of Hittite inscriptions.

D

CHAPTER III

THE TELL-EL-AMARNA TABLETS.—In 1887 an
Egyptian woman, digging for earth for her garden,
found at Tell-el-Amarna, about 300 kilometres
south of Cairo, a number of inscribed clay tablets.
They were soon dispersed among the European
Museums, London and Berlin now possessing most of
them. They proved to be letters in cuneiform
script, for the most part in the Babylonian language,
from the kings of Syria and Palestine to the kings
of Egypt. Among them were also letters from
Babylonia, Assyria and Mitanni. These letters
establish synchronisms between the rulers of these
states which are invaluable for chronology, and
must be read in their entirety to get a clear view
of Egyptian diplomacy. Suffice it to say here that
Egypt was courted by these kings for the purpose
of obtaining rich treasures in exchange for native
productions, to cement alliances and to gain advan-
tages over their neighbours. As it happens, the
native sources for Babylonian history are very
fragmentary for this period, and scholars are by no

means agreed as to the order in which the ruling Kassite sovereigns of Babylonia should be arranged. On the other hand, the Egyptian monarchs are now dated with considerable certainty from Egyptian monuments.

In the time of Thothmes I. Egypt was already exerting her power in Mesopotamia, and Thothmes III. evidently exchanged presents with the king of Assyria. Assyria then fell under the power of Mitanni, but when it was once more independent, active correspondence with Egypt again went on.

The Tell-el-Amarna tablets further show the presence in Mesopotamia of the Aramæans, whose earlier branches appear as Akhlamê and Suti. Their nationality was primarily Semitic; they called their settlements *Beth*, and the people *marî* or *Benê*. Thus the tribe who gave the name to Bît Adini, or *Beth Eden*, would be called *mâr Adini* or *Bene Eden*. They seem to have been pastoral folk whose incursions filled up the open land and, of course, ruined the towns. But, in course of time, they settled into town dwellers. From their nomadic habits they were very difficult to check, and ultimately formed very powerful communities. Aramaic became the language of a large part of Mesopotamia.

The kingdom of Mitanni appears to have been founded by a branch of the so-called Hittite people, with whom the rulers of Egypt early came in contact. It has recently been brought into prominence by the discovery of many documents at Boghaz-koi, in the district of Pteria, written in the cuneiform character, and containing important despatches from Mitanni to Hittite kings.

We know from the Babylonian Chronicles that the Hittites invaded Babylonia in the reign of Samsuditana, last king of the First Dynasty, and the Kassites who founded the so-called Third Dynasty of Babylon may have been part of these Hittite peoples. At any rate one of the semi-independent kingdoms of this folk was situated about Malatia, and, known to its own people as the kingdom of Mitanni, played a great part in Assyrian history as the kingdom of Khani or Khanigalbat. It seems to have been established at least as early as Hammurabi's time. Thothmes III. mentions Mitanni.

We know now the names of at least six Mitanni kings. They all bore names which have a strong likeness to Aryan names; and among their gods were Indra, Varuna, and Mithra, which are clearly Aryan. Hence it is clear that there were Aryan elements in the population of Mitanni, and apparently in power. The people are referred to as Kharri, in which name some see the name Aryan. How far the Assyrian people were affected by this conquest

LETTER FROM TUSHRATTA TO AMENOPHIS III.

is difficult to say, but their early conflicts with
such warrior folk must have helped to form their
national character.

The letter of Tushratta to Amenophis IV., king
of Egypt, proposing to send Ishtar of Nineveh to
Egypt to heal the king of his sickness, has long been
taken as implying the dependence of Assyria, or
at least of Nineveh, upon Mitanni.   The so-called
Hittite tablets excavated by Professor Winckler
at Boghaz-koï, have thrown more light upon the
matter.   Mattiuza, son, and second on the throne
after Tushratta, together with his overlord, Sub-
biluliuma of Khatti, by their inscriptions establish
the following facts :—

1. The Assyrians had once been vassals of
Mattiuza's forefathers.

2. Saushatar, Mattiuza's great great grandfather, had carried off a quantity of gold and silver
from Asshur, which city he must have captured.

3. After the death of Tushratta the Assyrians
and men of Alshe had divided his lands.   The
Assyrians were then independent.   It was Ashur-
uballit who, like Tushratta, was contemporary
with Amenophis IV., and who, as Adad-nirari I. tells
us, destroyed the army of the Shubarî, an old term
for Mesopotamian peoples.

Now in Ashur-uballit's letter to Egypt, he states
that since his ancestor Ashur-nâdin-akhê sent an

embassy to Egypt, no one had gone to Egypt
from Khanigalbat or Mitanni. This means that,
as vassal of Mitanni, no Assyrian ruler could send
an embassy on his own account to Egypt, partly
because it would be a claim to independence, partly
because Mitanni held the roads. Consequently
we must put the ancestor Ashur-nâdin-akhê before
the Mitanni conquest, *i.e.* before Saushatar.

Now we have been able to extract from the new
Hittite documents with certainty the following
table of rulers of Mitanni :—

> (1) Saushatar.
> (2) Artatama I.
> (3) Sutarna I.

(4) Artashshumara.   (5) Tushratta.   Artatama II.
                  (7) Mattiuza.   (6) Sutarna II.
                              Aitakama.

Of these, Tushratta was contemporary of Amenophis IV., 1379-1362 B.C., and of Amenophis III.,
1414-1379 B.C. His father, Sutarna, married his
daughter, Gilu-Khipa, to Amenophis III. His
grandfather, Artatama, married his daughter to
Thothmes IV., 1423-1414 B.C. Artatama's father,
Saushatar, must have been contemporary with
Amenophis II., 1449-1423 B.C., perhaps a year or

two with Thothmes III. As Thothmes IV. only reigned nine years or so, Artatama's reign might well have fallen partly in that of Amenophis II.

Now we put Ashur-nâdin-akhê at least partly before Saushatar, and his reign may well have overlapped Thothmes III., 1501-1447. It was in his twenty-third year that Thothmes III. recorded the receipt from a prince of Asshur of costly gifts, three great blocks of fine lapis lazuli, and three pieces of precious stone from Babylon. It is then natural to suppose that Ashur-nâdin-akhê was the king who received twenty talents of gold from Egypt, and we may date him about 1478 B.C. Of course the evidence is still slight and needs inscriptional confirmation.

It may well be that this conquest of Assyria extended to Babylonia. For thence the images of Marduk and his consort, Zarpanît, were carried off to Mitanni. Were the Kassites really from Mitanni? We can now return to the rulers of Asshur. The kings we have to name may have been subject to Mitanni for a few generations, or they may have been gradually recovering from the conquest and its consequences. Ashur-nâdin-akhê probably reigned before the conquest, but whether it occurred in his reign or on his death or under one of his successors, we cannot yet decide.

ASHUR-NÂDIN-AKHI I. is named as his " father " by Ashur-uballit in a letter addressed to Amenophis IV., discovered in the archives of the kings of Egypt at Tell-el-Amarna. Ashur-uballit further states that earlier relations existed between the kings of Egypt and Assyria. Now Kadashman-Bêl, the king of Babylon, sent to Amenophis III. of Egypt four letters, preserved in the same archive. They do not, however, throw much light on Assyrian history. Kurigalzu, king of Babylon, is mentioned in these letters as on good terms with the king of Egypt, and his son, Burnaburiash, king of Babylon, refers to the Assyrians as his subjects, and protests against an embassy from them having been received in Egypt. He asks that Assyria shall gain no advantage to his detriment. We may regard his attitude to Assyria as merely diplomatic. The claim to be overlord is not supported by any other indication. Burnaburiash was succeeded by his son, Karakhardash, who married Muballitat-sherûa, the daughter of Ashur-uballit, and, according to the *Synchronous History*, Karakhardash and Ashur-uballit renewed the boundary treaty of their forefathers.

It is probable that when Ashur-uballit calls Ashur-nâdin-akhi his father he is only following a custom common enough to indicate an ancestor. Ashur-uballit may quite well have meant that Ashur-nâdin-akhi was a former ruler, who was known to the Egyptian king as having had relations with Egypt.

ASHUR-BÊL-NISHÊSHU   II. — The   *Synchronous History* records that a king of Assyria of this name made a treaty with Karaindash, king of Karduniash. Assyria was therefore again on terms of equality with Babylonia. The presumption is that the country was recovering from the effects of the Mitanni conquest. Adad-nirari I. speaks of a monarch of this name who restored or completed the work done by Puzur-Ashir I. on the walls of the " new city " at Asshur. Probably it also was rendered necessary by the Mitanni conquest.

PUZUR-ASHUR II.—We know from the *Synchronous History* that a king of Assyria of this name made a treaty with Burnaburiash, king of Karduniash. He therefore follows Ashur-bêl-nishêshu. We do not know at what interval, but as the next king of Assyria named in the *Synchronous History* is Ashur-uballit, whose father and grandfather we know, we must place Puzur-Ashur II. before them.

ASHUR-NADIN-AKHI II.—Known from his grandson's inscriptions only.

ERBA-ADAD I.—He is known from his son's inscriptions. He has also left a very fragmentary inscription of his own, in which he claims to be *shar kishshati*, and therefore may be presumed to have held possession of Haran. He further styles himself " king of the four quarters " of the world, which usually implied lordship over Babylonia also. He

may be presumed, therefore, to have brought a
war with that country to a successful conclusion.
The references which later kings make to repairs
at the *Bît pagri* " cemetery," or Mausoleum of
Erba-Adad, possibly refer to the enclosure in
Asshur next the walls of the city where were found
the *stelæ* of the Assyrian kings and governors of
Assyria. There were two rows of them. The royal
monuments were at least twenty-five in number,
fifteen of limestone, five of alabaster and five of basalt.
They bore inscriptions of which some are still legible,
and give the names of Adad-nirari I., Shalmaneser I.,
Tukulti-Ninib I., Ashur-resh-ishi II., Tiglath-pileser
III., Shalmaneser II., Shamshi-Adad VI., Sammuramat, the queen, Sennacherib, and others less
well preserved. It must have represented the
Sepulchres of the Kings. Other kings were buried
at Nineveh. The row south of these were apparently
all set up for city governors. Ten have been recovered, of which eight had places for inscriptions.
Unfortunately these cannot yet be dated, but the
titles borne by some of them illustrate the extent
of Assyrian rule in their days.

Thus Ilu-ittia was *shaknu* or viceroy of Asshur,
of Kar-Tukulti-Ninib, of Êkallate, of Itu and
Ruquhku. Marduk-ishmeani was viceroy of
Nairi. Nishpatti-utli was viceroy of Asshur and
Kalah. Shamash-bêl-utsur was viceroy of Kalah,

Amedi, Singani and Ialuna. Adad-bêl-ukin was viceroy of Kar-Tukulti-Ninib, of Êkallate and Ruqukhu. Bêl-uballit was Tartan, surveyor of the temples, Vizier, viceroy of Tabit, Haran, and Khuzirina. Great was their honour to be buried with the kings.

ASHUR-UBALLIT.—This king in his letters to the Egyptian king names as his ancestor Ashur-nâdin-akhi I. In the so-called well inscription at Asshur this king gives his own father's name as Erba-Adad, and Ashur-nâdin-akhi (II.) as that of his grandfather. The well was made by the latter and repaired by Ashur-uballit. A repair made so soon speaks for some wilful destruction, and makes it possible that Asshur had suffered a capture, perhaps under Erba-Adad. Shalmaneser I. records that an Ashur-uballit had rebuilt at Nineveh a temple of Nineveh built by one Shamshi-Adad. Here again the fall of a temple may be due to the capture of Nineveh. An Assyrian king who held Nineveh could hardly leave the temple of its city god long in ruins. It can hardly be that Ashur-uballit had to rebuild a temple in Nineveh and unstop (?) a well in his own city, except in consequence of a recent siege and capture of both cities.

Adad-nirari I. says of his grandfather's father, Ashur-uballit, that he was a mighty king, whose priesthood in the temples was glorious, whose

prosperity was made pure for ever, who broke up
the forces of the widespread Shubarî (a name for
the N.W. district) and enlarged border and frontier.

His relationships with Babylon were peculiar and
complicated. We have noted that his daughter
married Karakhardash, who came to the throne
in Babylon. Ashur-uballit had already had relations with his father. On Karakhardash's death,
the son of this marriage, Kadashman-kharbe, came
to the throne. Apparently Ashur-uballit assisted him
in clearing the Euphrates caravan road of the Suti
bandits, whom he had denounced to Amenophis
IV., as infesting the roads to the West. This inter-
ference may have provoked the Kassite aristocracy,
who, at any rate, revolted against Kadashman-
kharbe, and put him to death. They set a Kassite
Nazibugash on the throne. Ashur-uballit marched
into Babylonia and put the usurper to death. He
then placed Kurigalzu II., a mere child, on the
throne. He may have been the son of the murdered
Kadashman-kharbe, or a brother. Though he
probably started with Assyrian support, he lived
to reign fifty-five years. Ashur-uballit, his grandfather, or perhaps great grandfather, cannot long
have survived his accession.

BÊL-NIRARI.—Bêl-nirari, in any case, was the son
of Ashur-uballit, and succeeded him. He clearly
inherited the Assyrian enmity for the Kassites,

for his grandson, Adad-nirari I., ascribes to him the conquest of the hordes of Kassites, perhaps in their mountain home, and says that he conquered all his enemies and enlarged boundary and territory. It is very probable that he did this in alliance with Kurigalzu himself.. But later he fought with Kurigalzu at Sugagi, on the Tsal-tsallat river. He defeated the Babylonian with great slaughter, and made a fresh delimitation of boundaries.

ARIK-DÊN-ILU.—Bel-nirari's son succeeded him. His name has usually been read Pu-di-ilu, in ignorance of the fact that *Pu* and *Di* were ideograms. From one of his inscriptions his fuller name may have been Arik-dên-Bêl. Fragments of his annals record indications of at least five campaigns, one against Iasubakula, very likely the Iasubigalli of Sennacherib's time, whom, with the Kassites, he regarded as having been previously invincible. Another campaign was against the land Nigimti, where Adad-nirari I. also warred, where he names a city Arnûni. A third names the cities Kutila, Kudina, Tarbilu and Namu-bilkhi. A fourth names Halah, near the Chabur, and probably points to the possession of Haran. Everywhere he conquered his enemies, and records rich spoil, chiefly sheep and cattle as brought to Asshur. In one case he names 250,000 people, possibly as captives. The last campaign speaks of the rebellion of one Asini.

His son, Adad-nirari I., credits him with having conquered the land of Turûkî and Nigimti as well as all the kings of the mountains and hills, the Qutî, Akhlame and Sutî as well as the Iauri and their lands, and thus enlarging boundary and territory. He was evidently a great conqueror. His relations with Babylon seem to have been pacific.

ADAD-NIRARI I.—Adad-nirari I. makes a good impression on our minds because he is so careful to ascribe their rightful dues to his forefathers. He took up the tale of their conquests and carried it on with his own. He went further still, to the Lullumi in the east. For some reason which we cannot yet fathom, war broke out with Nazi-marattash, king of Babylon, and Adad-nirari I. was able to claim the victory and dictate new boundaries. Here the boundary ran from the land of Pilasqi to the Lullumi. He boasts of having rebuilt the cities of the Kassites, Qutî, Lullumi and Shubarî folk, and defeated all the people from Lubdi and Rapiqu to Elukhat. He also appears to have taken Haran, with which agrees the title, *shar kishshâti*, which he bears. He repaired the walls of the palace which Ashur-nâdin-akhi, his forefather had built, and a shrine in the temple of Asshur. The *mushlala* of the temple of Ashur, a covered corridor or portico, the quay wall along the bank of the Tigris, a dam to turn the waters

round the south walls, and other buildings in Asshur
and Nineveh are associated with his name.

SHALMANESER I. (*circa* 1300 B.C.).—The throne
passed from Adad-nirari I. to his son, Shalmaneser
I., and Assyria entered definitely upon a career of
western conquest. The king crossed the Tigris in
its upper course, planted a strong military colony
on the Kashiari range near Diabekr, and then proceeded along the southern spurs of the mountains
west to Malatia. The fragments of his annals give
three campaigns in this region, in which he plundered
eight lands, one so utterly that he " collected its
dust and poured it out at the doors of the temples "
in Asshur. His second campaign was to Khanigalbat, the old Mitanni. Here the king, Sattuara,
offered stout resistance. He had allied himself
with the farther Hittites and the Aramaic Akhlamū.
Shalmaneser, however, overcame all opposition,
and, driving his foes before him, ravaged and
plundered the allies up to Carchemish on the
Euphrates. It is interesting and most valuable
for ancient geography to follow his route, detailed
with the precision of a road-map, " from the city
Taiki up to the city Irridu on the slopes of Mount
Kashiari, to the city Elukhat, etc., etc." Sûti
nomads had settled in the district of which Haran
was capital. The Aramæans were gradually dis-
possessing the old settled inhabitants ; perpetual

tribal raids, and incessant petty wars made the
country an easy prey to the Assyrians, in whose
military rule and strict order lay the only hope of
the discordant elements of population ever settling
down into anything like a nation. Assyria was
not yet populous enough to police all Mesopotamia,
but by perpetually exacting tribute and forbidding
internecine war, it kept the country in some order.
The Shubarî and Lullumî were conquered in this
reign.

This extension of territory to North and North-
West made it difficult to rule from the ancient capital
at Asshur, so far south, perpetually necessitating
a crossing of the Tigris. So Shalmaneser built
a palace at Kalah and made a great city there,
forty miles farther up the Tigris, in the fork between
it and the upper Zab.

In Shalmaneser's reign, probably at its commencement, the great temple of Ashur in Asshur was
burnt down, apparently in consequence of an
earthquake, and he rebuilt it. He also restored the
temple of Ishtar at Nineveh, which had fallen
from the same cause.

TUKULTI-NINIB I. (*circa* 1275 B.C.).—Shalmaneser
I. was succeeded by his son, Tukulti-Ninib I. We
are fortunate in possessing very full annals of his
reign. It is probable that his expeditions are not
related in chronological order, but grouped more

or less geographically. In his first year he tells us
that he conquered the chief N. and N.E. lands
and henceforth received annual tribute from them
at Asshur. Then he plundered and subdued the
N.W. regions of Mesopotamia up to Commagene.
This involved difficult marches among hills and over
passes all but impassable. The challenge thus made
to his northern neighbours could not be ignored,
and a powerful coalition was formed against him.
After sanguinary contests the forty kings of the
Nairi district were subjected to a perpetual tribute.

The king of Babylonia, Kashtiliash II., was the
next victim. Tukulti-Ninib marched into Babylonia and hemmed in its army. He forced a battle,
took Kashtiliash prisoner, and carried him in chains
to Asshur. Then he conquered the whole of
Babylonia, Sumer and Akkad, down to the Sealand.

For seven years Tukulti-Ninib ruled Babylonia,
apparently through various puppet kings. He not
only carried off its king, but even more serious,
its national god, Marduk, also. He plundered the
great temple of Esagila, in Babylon. Shagaraktishuriash, the last king of Babylon, had claimed
the title of *Shar kishshati*, and Tukulti-Ninib carried
off to Babylon this king's seal bearing that title.

Tukulti-Ninib had conceived the idea of building
an entire new city and calling it after his own name,
Kar-Tukulti-Ninib. He built there a temple for

E

Ashur and his great gods. He provided it with a canal, which shows that it was not far from the river. There he raised a platform of earth, confined by brick facings. Upon it he built his mighty palace, and surrounded the new city with a wall.

After his seven years' rule over Babylonia, the nobles of Akkad and Karduniash revolted and set up Adad-shum-utsur as king. In Assyria too, his own son, Ashur-natsir-pal, and the nobles of Assyria rebelled. They besieged him in his mighty house in Kar-Tukulti-Ninib, and slew him there.

ASHUR-NATSIR-PAL I.—There is no reason to think that this parricide did not succeed his father, but at present we are without monuments of his reign. For nearly a century the history becomes obscure once more, only a few incidents being made out with some certainty.

ASHUR-NIRARI III. and NABÛ-DÂN.—A letter preserved in the Kouyunjik Collections in the British Museum is addressed by one Adad-shum-utsur, king of Babylon, to two rulers of Assyria, who seem to have reigned together. They are called Ashur-nirari and Nabû-dân.

NINIB-TUKULTI-ASHUR and ADAD-SHUM-LISHIR.— The *Babylonian Chronicle*, after relating the murder of Tukulti-Ninib I. by his son, Ashur-natsir-pal I., goes on to say that for some sixteen years, Bêl, *i.e.* the statue of Marduk, remained in Assyria,

STATUE OF ASHUR-NATSIR-PAL I.

but in the time of Tukulti-Asshur, Bêl came back
to Babylon. There is no Babylonian king of such
a name as Tukulti-Ashur. In the letter of Adad-
shum-utsur, mention is made of unrest in Assyria,
and reference to a certain Adad-shum-lishir.

Now there is another letter preserved in the
Kouyunjik Collections, addressed to some one in
power in Assyria, by a king of Babylonia, in which
he repels all proffered friendship. He points out
that a king of Assyria, by name Ninib-tukulti-
Ashur, of which name Tukulti-Ashur is an allowable
abbreviation, has fled to Babylon leaving his representative, Adad-shum-lishir, to rule Assyria.
The rebels in Assyria had described Ninib-tukulti-
Ashur as a weak, unmanly ruler. We may conclude,
from a comparison of these passages, that Ninib-
tukulti-Ashur was a king of Assyria, and that Ashur-
nirari III. and Nabû-dân had rebelled against him
in his absence and expelled his viceroy, or successor,
Adad-shum-lishir. They then approached the
king of Babylon, whether with a view to the ex-
tradition of the fugitives or their assassination
does not appear, and added threats because their
proposals were not complied with.

We may further conclude that whether Ninib-
tukulti-Ashur had fled from a rebellion, or made a
friendly journey to return Marduk's statue, he at
any rate was protected in his exile by the king of

Babylon. It was probably he who also carried back to Babylon the seal of Shagaraktishuriash mentioned above, which Sennacherib once more brought back after 600 years, and regarded as having been "stolen."

Unfortunately we have no inscriptional evidence of the reigns of Ninib-tukulti-Ashur and Adad-shum-lishir, but we may provisionally place them before Ashur-nirari III. and Nabû-dân. The rule of these usurpers cannot have been long, for the reign of Adad-shum-utsur, which lasted only thirty years, has to include Bêl's captivity of sixteen years and the above events.

BÊL-KUDUR-UTSUR.—We next know of Bêl-kudur-utsur, who had apparently to meet Adad-shum-utsur in battle, and there lost his life. At present we have no other indication of his existence.

ERBA-ADAD II.—Only known as father of Ninib-apil-esharra. He may not have been king.

NINIB-APIL-ESHARRA.—The *Synchronous History* states that Ninib-apil-esharra returned to Assyria after the battle in which Bêl-kudur-utsur lost his life. Adad-shum-utsur followed him up and besieged him in Asshur. The Babylonians are not said to have taken Asshur, nor, on the other hand, to have suffered any defeat. That Ninib-apil-esharra was not able to meet them on his frontier points to the weakness of Assyria, which is confirmed by the fact that the titles of the Babylonian kings,

since Tukulti-Ninip's fall, indicate their possessing
Mesopotamia. Tiglath-pileser I. names Ninib-apil-
esharra as his ancestor, and calls him a powerful
king, beloved of Ashur, who truly shepherded the
hosts of Assyria.

ASHUR-DÂN I.—Ashur-dân I., son of Ninib-apil-
esharra, soon made headway against Babylonia.
He reconquered the regions beyond the Zab. He
invaded Karduniash and took Zaban, Irria and
Akarsallu, and carried off rich booty to Asshur.
Tiglath-pileser I. says that he lived to be an old man,
and took down the temple of Ashur with intent to
rebuild it, but did not do so.

MUTAKKIL-NUSKU.—This king was son of Ashur-
dân I. He is named by his son and successor, Ashur-
rêsh-ishi, and by his grandson, Tiglath-pileser I.,
but nothing more is yet known of him.

ASHUR-RÊSH-ISHI I.—This king, son of Mutakkil-
Nusku, is described by his son, Tiglath-pileser I., as a
mighty king who conquered hostile lands and subdued
all the proud. From fragments of his own inscriptions we learn that he destroyed the wide spreading
hosts of the Akhlamî, reduced again the Lullumî,
the whole of the Kutî and their mountain fastnesses.
The *Synchronous History* tells us that Nebuchadrezzar I., king of Babylon, invaded Assyria, and laid
siege to Zanqî, one of the Assyrian fortresses. Ashur-
rêsh-ishi assembled his chariots and started to raise

the siege. Nebuchadrezzar apparently was en-
cumbered by his siege-trains, so burnt them and
retreated in good order. He returned with fresh
forces and a new siege-train and marched against
the fortress to take it. Again, Ashur-rêsh-ishi sent
chariots and infantry, and joined battle. The
Assyrians won with a great slaughter, plundered the
Babylonian camp, captured forty chariots and their
trappings, and took prisoner the leader of the forces!
Further, we read of buildings and restorations at the
temples of Ashur, Ishtar and Irnina.

CHAPTER IV

ASSYRIA AS A WORLD POWER

TIGLATH-PILESER I., the son of Ashur-rêsh-ishi, is very noteworthy on many accounts. His great prism inscription is interesting because it was selected in the early days of cuneiform decipherment as a test of the ability of scholars to read Assyrian. Many copies were produced, four of which were buried, one at each of the corners of the great temple of Anu and Adad, in the city of Asshur.

This prism inscription contains accounts of his first five campaigns. In his accession year he demonstrated in force against Muskhu, the Meshech of the Old Testament, on the borders of Cappadocia and Commagene. In the first year of his reign he attacked the Shubarî, where he met and overthrew 4000 Hittites, and captured 120 chariots. Then 20,000 men of the Muskhu and five kings who had held for fifty years the lands of Alzi and Purukuzzu, which had been subject to Assyria in Tukulti-Ninib's time, came down and raided Commagene. Tiglath-pileser gathered his chariots and militia and attacked through the Kashiari hills. He met the foe in Commagene and overwhelmed them. He took 6000 prisoners and immense booty. He then marched through the length and breadth of the land, exacted tribute and plundered the rebels. He burnt and razed to the ground many cities. A remnant fled across the Tigris to the city Shereshe and held out there. Tiglath-pileser stormed it. The Qurtê came to the assistance of Commagene: he defeated them with great slaughter. He captured Kili-Teshup, son of Kali-Teshup, and carried off his wives and family with great spoil. He burnt the city and its palace. Urrartinash, a stronghold on Mount Panarus, was captured, and its inhabitants fled to the mountains. Shadi-Teshup, son of Khatu-sar, submitted. Tiglath-pileser took his sons hostages and again carried off great spoil. Tiglath-pileser spared his life, but laid a heavy tribute upon him for the future.

A minor expedition, with thirty chariots and some veterans, was directed against Mildish, which involved that the king should often journey on foot, so at Mount Aruma he left his chariots and led his men " like a lion." The place was captured and the land ravaged.

Four thousand men of Kashi and Urume, Hittite soldiers who had revolted and seized the cities of the Shubarî, submitted. Tiglath-pileser took them, with their chariots, and added them to his army. Thus reinforced, he attacked Commagene once more, ravaged the whole land and annexed it. In his next

EIGHT-SIDED PRISM OF TIGLATH-PILESER I.

campaign he took a new route, and devastated the lands of Khania and the Qurtê. They made a stand on Mount Azu, but were defeated with great slaughter. He captured twenty-five cities at the foot of the mountains. The people of Adaush fled, but came back and submitted and were put under tribute. The lands of Saraush and Ammaush, formerly unconquered, were devastated. A similar fate overtook the lands of Isua and Daria. Then he crossed the lower Zab and captured Murattash and Saradaush, on the slopes of Mounts Asaniu and Atuma, acquiring great spoil. Next the land of Sugi, in Kirkhi, where 6000 of the enemy, all mountaineers, who had to be attacked on foot, were conquered and their lands devastated. Some submitted and were held to tribute.

In the next campaign he went to the lands of the distant kings on the shore of the Upper Sea. He enumerates sixteen difficult mountains to be surmounted. He used his chariots where possible, then went forward on foot. He made bridges with tree trunks where necessary. But he conquered in spite of all, and enumerates twenty-three kings of the Nairi land as conquered. Sixty kings of Nairi land were pursued even to the Upper Sea. He spared the lives of the kings, made them swear fidelity, took their sons as hostages, and laid a tribute of 1200 horses and 2000 head of cattle upon them. One king, Sieni

of Daieni, who was obstinate, was taken to Asshur
as prisoner, but released on becoming a worshipper
of the Assyrian gods. A noteworthy incident was
an expedition to Milidia, capital of the old Mitanni
district of Khanigalbat. It submitted and was
spared and subjected to a yearly tribute.

The next campaign was directed across the desert
against the Akhlamî and other Aramæans. From
Sukhi to Carchemish Tiglath-pileser rushed by a
forced march : it was a lightning swoop and produced much spoil. The inhabitants took to the
water and swam the Euphrates. Tiglath-pileser
pursued them in boats. Then he raided and burnt
six cities at the foot of Mount Beshri. Once more
Asshur was glutted with spoil.

Tiglath-pileser then forced his way among the
mountains of the North. The Mutsri, as usual, were
reinforced by the Qumanî, but Tiglath-pileser's
tactics were too clever. Into one city, Arini, he
managed to shepherd them all, and shut them up.
They could not stand a siege, and so submitted. He
spared their lives, took hostages, and laid tribute on
them. The Mutsri then called out all their forces to
check the invader, and he met 20,000 on Mount Tala
and put them to flight. He pursued the remnant
beyond their own frontiers. The strong fortress of
Khunusa was destroyed, and a curious monument
set up. Tiglath-pileser erected a tower of burnt

brick on which he placed a decree on a bronze plate
to the effect that the city should never be reinhabited,
and its walls never rebuilt. It further recorded the
conquests he had made, and the spoil which he had
captured. Next, the capital of the Qumanî, in which
had taken refuge the king and three hundred
families of rebels, was invested and taken. Tiglath-
pileser spared their lives, took hostages, and increased
taxation. Thus he had subdued forty-two lands and
their princes from beyond the lower Zab to the
farther side of the Euphrates, the land of the Hittites
and the Upper Sea of the West, by the fifth year
of his reign. His purpose was, as he says, to place
them under one rule, literally "to make them of one
tongue," and put a stop to their incessant internecine
wars and continual raids upon his territory.

On the same prism he records his exploits as a
hunter. The huge wild ox, or buffalo, which still
roamed the open lands in Mitanni, was evidently a
trophy to be proud of, and near Araziqu, close to the
Hittite land, he killed four and brought their hides
and horns to Asshur. In the country of Haran and
the district of the Habur he killed ten mighty bull
elephants and took their tusks and hides, with four
live elephants, to Asshur. He boasts of having killed
120 lions on foot, and as many as 800 in his hunting
chariot. All sorts of beasts of the field and birds of
heaven he hunted and killed.

His building efforts were noteworthy. The temples of Ishtar of Asshur, of Martu, of the old Bêl, and of other gods, which had fallen in Asshur, he rebuilt. He restored the palaces of his forefathers all over the land : renewed the walls of cities and set to work the *shadufs* all over the country. He stored up grain, collected huge herds of horses, cattle and asses from the conquered lands, and preserved for hunting large numbers of deer, stags, ibex, and wild goats, as if they were sheep. He made plantations and parks, and filled them with rare trees and plants. His chariots and cavalry were organised and kept in perpetual readiness.

From the same prism we have already often quoted his genealogical notices of his predecessors and the chronological data for the history of the temple of Anu and Adad, which he completely rebuilt. This was commenced at the very beginning of his reign, and took five years to complete, with a solidity and magnificence hitherto unparalleled. The great treasure-house of Adad was rebuilt and filled with spoils from his many conquests. With the usual prayers for blessings on his reign, and on the pious successors who should preserve his memorials, and with curses on those who destroyed or defaced them, this superb inscription concludes.

From some of his other inscriptions we may add a few details. In his later years he made an expedition to Arime, and to towns in the district of Dûr-Kurigalzu, in Babylonia, and captured a viceroy called Karaburiash. His career of conquest and annexation, with consequent transportation of peoples and accumulation of spoil, continued. Lastly, he went to sea in the ships of Arvad and slew a mighty dolphin; afterwards he set up at Asshur huge basalt representations of these dolphins. The king of Mutsrê, probably Egypt, sent him a huge crocodile, which he exhibited in Assyria. This unfortunately badly damaged and broken record, which once dated each military event by year and month, if not also day, devotes four columns to the above details and begins the fifth with a reference to Akkad.

The *Synchronous History* relates that Tiglath-pileser, king of Assyria, and Marduk-nâdin-akhê, king of Babylonia, " for a second time " set in array their chariots above the lower Zab, over against Arzukhina. In the second year they fought at Marriti, which is above the land of Akkad, and Tiglath-pileser captured Dûr-Kurigalzu and Sippar of Shamash, Sippar of Anunitum, Babylon, and Opis, and took away their fortifications. He further plundered Akarsallu up to Lubdi, and subdued all the land of Sukhi to Rapiqu. The reference to " a second time " is explained by the fact that although the *Synchronous History* does not record it, Tiglath-pileser was the loser in the first conflict, doubtless because his troops were largely occupied elsewhere. Marduk-nâdin-akhê had invaded Assyria and carried off Adad and Shala, gods of Ekallâte to Babylon.

In Asshur, Tiglath-pileser built several palace courts, called after the costly woods with which they were furnished—the cedar house, the boxwood house, the tamarisk house, etc. He repaired the canal cut by Ashur-dân I., in which no water had flowed for thirty years. The Mausoleum of Erba-Adad I., and the great north terrace which Ashur-nâdin-akhê had built, were restored. The moat of Asshur had been ruined and blocked up with earth, and was now cleaned out from the Tigris to the Gurgurri gates. These gates were renewed and covered with bronze plates. The wall of Asshur was renewed and faced with a rampart of earth. The Quay wall along the Tigris was restored from the water level and made secure with brick set in asphalt. The great terrace of the new palace which Tukulti-Ninip I. had built was made new. He built a palace in a city at the beginning of the road from Asshur ; and the old palace of Ashur-rêsh-ishi at Apki was renewed.

ASHUR-BÊL-KALA.—This king was the son of Tiglath-pileser I., and probably succeeded his father. Apparently he left no issue, for he was succeeded by his brother, Shamshi-Adad VI., whose son succeeded him. The *Synchronous History* relates that Marduk-shapik-zêr-mâti formed an alliance with him. When

THE SYNCHRONOUS HISTORY.

this monarch fled and Adad-apli-iddina, an upstart, was made king, Ashur-bêl-kala married his daughter and took her with a rich dowry to Assyria. A very singular nude female statue, probably a goddess, was found at Nineveh, with an inscription showing that it belonged to the palace of Ashur-bêl-kala. Another inscription occurs on a fragment of a colossus or guardian deity for a palace gate found at Asshur.

SHAMSHI-ADAD VI.—We possess some fragmentary inscriptions showing that he restored temples in Assyria, and amongst them a temple of Ishtar at Nineveh.

ASHUR-NATSIR-PAL II. was the son of Shamshi-Adad VI., and father of Shalmaneser II., who succeeded him.

SHALMANESER II. was the son of Ashur-natsir-pal II. His stele was set up in Asshur.

TIGLATH-PILESER II.—Perhaps we may put here Tiglath-pileser II., son of Adad-nirari II., who adorned the *kigallu* of the temple of Ashur in Asshur.

ASHUR-RABI II.—He is known as the father of Ashur-rêsh-ishi II., who followed him. He may be referred to by Shalmaneser III. ; see under Adad-nirari III. below.

ASHUR-RÊSH-ISHI II.—This son of Ashur-rabi succeeded him, and was followed by Tiglath-pileser III.

TIGLATH-PILESER III.—He is known as the son of Ashur-rêsh-ishi II., and was followed by Ashur-dân III.

ASHUR-DÂN III.—He was the son of Tiglath-pileser III., and was followed by Adad-nirari III.

The *Eponym Canon* now commences and enables us accurately to date the accessions of each king down to Ashur-bânipal.

ADAD-NIRARI III., B.C. 911—890.—This king has left a record of repairs which he made at the old Quay of Asshur built by Adad-nirari I., son of Arik-dên-ilu. He calls himself son of Ashur-dân.   He is also known by an inscription cut on a cylindrical object of black basalt which once stood on a square base, and merely gives his genealogy.   The *Synchronous History* now begins again to take up the tale of Assyrian successes. We may take it that its silence since Ashur-bêl-kala means that Assyria had suffered an eclipse of power. The Aramæan tribes, according to Shalmaneser IV., had taken Pitru and Mutkinu, which had been annexed by Tiglath-pileser I.   This they did in the reign of an Ashur-rabbi, who probably was Ashur-rabi II.   A king, Ashur-irbi, set up an image of himself in the mountains of Northern Syria, near the Amanus range, which shows that he carried out successfully an expedition to the Mediterranean coast.   That is scarcely consistent with want of success against the Aramæans, and it seems therefore best to identify him with Ashur-rabi I., despite the difference in the spelling of the name.

Of Adad-nirari III. we learn from the *Synchronous History* that he defeated two successive kings of Babylonia. Shamash-mudammiq set his army in battle array against Assyria, at the foot of Mount Ialman. Adad-nirari defeated him and captured his chariots. Then Nabû - shum - ishkun slew Shamash-mudammiq and reigned over Babylon. He soon had to reckon with Adad-nirari, who defeated him with heavy slaughter, captured many cities and great spoil. Having thus vindicated his claim to respect, Adad-nirari entered into alliance with Nabû-shum-ishkun, and each gave the other his daughter in marriage. Once more Asshur and Akkad were in close friendship.

TUKULTI-NINIP II., B.C. 890-885.—He succeeded his father Adad-nirari III., and was a really great conqueror. We only know details of five campaigns. His annals were drawn up in the most precise manner. Each march is set out from start to finish. In his last year, he started on the river Tartar, which runs down from the Sindjar range just west of the Euphrates and loses itself in the steppe. He had of course arrived there from Asshur, through his own land. He followed the river to its mouth, where he had a waterless desert before him. He struck off east to the Tigris. Here he was in Baby-

F

lonian territory, and he turned south to Dûr-Kurigalzu and on to Sippar. Then he turned backwards
up the Euphrates to the mouth of the Habur. Here
he found the asphalt springs of Hit. He names
place after place on the route, Khindani, Laqê,
Sirku, and Sûru. Then he traversed Bît-Khalupi,
Shadikani, and reached Nisibis. In the north
he came across the Muski. Then we have a record
of many buildings, especially the city wall of
Asshur, and the platform of a royal palace there.
Unfortunately, we possess only a fragmentary record
of this reign. He appears to have kept the peace
with Babylonia.

CHAPTER V

THE SECOND EMPIRE

ASHUR-NATSIR-PAL III., B.C. 885—860.—Apparently the capital had been moved to Nineveh. But from the sixth year onwards Ashur-natsir-pal started on his expeditions from Kalah. In the mounds of its modern site at Nimroud were found the magnificent sculptured slabs, or bas-reliefs, which are among the chief treasures of the British Museum. His annals were inscribed on the pavement of the entrance to the temple of Ninib at Kalah, and in shorter form on his great obelisk, but they are repeated on all sorts of monuments, colossal bulls and lions, memorial tablets, so-called clay bowls, bricks, an altar to Bêl, and a limestone statue of himself.

Ashur-natsir-pal seems to have ordered his palaces to be covered with inscriptions, but the workmen employed did so with small care for sense. They took as model one short inscription and repeated it endlessly. It is known as the Standard Inscription.

Ashur-natsir-pal says that he found Kalah a heap

of ruined buildings and mounds. He rebuilt it, and peopled it from the lands he had conquered, from Sukhi, Laqê, Sirku, beyond the Euphrates, from Zamûa, Bît Adini, and the Hittite lands Liburna and Patini. He dug out a canal from the upper Zab and called it Pati-Khegalli, and planted gardens round it. He improved the ancient mound, going down to the water-level and renewing its containing walls to the height of 120 courses of bricks. He rebuilt the city wall. He made palace halls of various choice woods. He set up white limestone images of great beasts of the mountains and the seas at the great gates. He filled his palaces with all kinds of rich treasures.

In his first year he went to Numme and captured the cities among the mountains. Next to Kirruri, where he received tribute. The distant Gilzani and Khubushki brought gifts. Then, by the pass of Khulun he went into Kirkhi and conquered the cities between the mountains. He flayed Bûbu, son of Bubâ, governor at Nishtun, after he had brought him back to Arbela. He set up an image of himself in Mount Egi, where he also founded a city, called after him. In that year, on the 24th of Ab, he went from Nineveh to the towns at the foot of Nipur and conquered them. Thence he crossed the Tigris and went on to Commagene, and there received its tribute and that of Mushku. Sûru in Bît-

Khalupi had revolted, slain its viceroy, and set up a pretender, Akhiababa, from Bît-Adini, as their king. Ashur-natsir-pal at once collected his forces and marched to the district of the Habur. On his way he received tribute from the cities of Shadikanni and Qatnu. The city fathers of Sûru gave themselves up. The upstart king was taken prisoner with all his supporters, the viceroy reinstated, and Ashur-natsir-pal stripped the city of its treasures. He flayed all the chief men who had revolted, and built a pillar at the city gate, which he covered with their skins. Some he walled up within the pillar, and some he impaled on stakes about it. Some he carried back to Assyria and flayed them there, as he did Akhiababa, and spread his skin upon the wall of Nineveh. In Sûru he received the tribute of Laqê and Khindanu.

In his own eponym year, B.C. 883, Ilu-ibni, governor of the Sukhi, came, in fear of his life, with his brethren and his sons to Nineveh to offer presents. Then Ashur-natsir-pal heard that the Assyrians whom Shalmaneser I. had settled in Khalzi-lukha had revolted and attacked Damdamusa, a royal city. He at once attacked them. On the way, at the source of the Subnat, where stood the images of Tiglath-pileser I. and Tukulti-Ninip I., he set up his own beside them. Tribute came from Isalla. He went up the Kashiari to Kinabu, the rebel head-

quarters, stormed it, and burned 3000 captives.
The governor, who had betrayed his trust, he took
alive, flayed him, and spread his skin on the walls
of Damdamusa, which he then burnt. Mariru
shared the same fate. The men of Nirbu had come
to assist the rebels and were defeated. A remnant
took refuge in Tela with its threefold walls. It was
stormed and utterly destroyed. He raided Nairi in
similar fashion. At Tushkha, which he captured, he
rebuilt the city, made a palace for himself in it, and
set up there his image. The old Assyrian settlers,
who had been reduced to ruin by want and hunger,
and had taken refuge in Shuprî, he brought back and
settled in Tushkha, which he made part of the royal
domain. The rest of Nirbu submitted. He received tribute from Bît Zamani, Shuprî, Nirdun,
Urume, and the kings of Nairi. He imposed forced
labour on these kings, probably to build his city
Tushkha. He then quelled another revolt in Nirbu.
Then he entered the pass of Buliani and marched
to the river Sugia, conquering the cities of Kirkhi,
which lay in his route. He came out by Ardupa.
There he received tribute from the Hittites and
Mitanni.

In the next year he heard of the revolt of Dagara
and its coalition with Zamûa. The rebels built a
wall to block the pass of Babite. Ashur-natsir-pal
attacked at once and carried all before him. He

captured the cities, forced the pass of Babite, and
went up Mount Nitsir. He captured the chief
towns and 150 villages. He set out from Tukulti-
Ashur-atsbat and scoured Mount Nispi.

In the next year he heard that Ameka and
Arashtua had discontinued their tribute. So the
third time he went to Zamûa. From Kakzi he crossed
the lower Zab, went up the pass of Babite, over the
Radanu river, to Mount Simaki. Then by a night
march he crossed the river Turnat and reached
Ammati, which he took as well as Kudun and twenty
cities round about it. Kisirtu and ten cities round
it fell. Bâra, Dûra, Bunisa, up to the pass of
Khashmar were destroyed. Then he reached
Zamri, the capital of Ameka. Ameka fled. The city
was plundered. Next Ashur-natsir-pal crossed the
river Lallu and up the Mount Etini, whither the
king had gone with his household and treasures.
These Ashur-natsir-pal captured. He crossed the
river Edir and hunted between the mountains of
Sû and Elaniu and brought back great spoil. The
chief cities with 150 villages were captured and
destroyed. Then he attacked other cities on Mount
Nispi. Here he received tribute from Sipirmena
" where the people speak like women." He next
had to cut a way through forests for his chariots,
and over the difficult Mount Lara came down to the
city Tukulti-Ashur-atsbat. The kings of Zamûa

in terror brought in tribute. He laid further taxes upon them and made them furnish labour for his buildings at Kalah. The people of Khuduni and Khartishi, Khubushki and Gilzani, brought tribute. Ashur-natsir-pal proceeded to clear the hills of fugitives. Mounts Aziru and Simaki had been their refuge, and a city called Mêsu. He slaughtered and plundered all over the districts. In the land of Zamûa he came upon Atlila, which had been the residence of Sibir, king of Karduniash, and was now a heap of ruins. Ashur-natsir-pal rebuilt it, fortified it, and made a palace there, more glorious than it had ever been. He called it Dûr-Ashur.

Next year he crossed the Tigris and entered Commagene. He consecrated a palace in Tulili and received tribute. Then he entered the pass of Ishtarâte and halted for tribute at Kibaki. Next he captured Matiati. Here he set up an image of himself. He camped at Zaza-bukha and received tribute from Kirkhi. Next he burnt Irria and received tribute from Sûru. Now he had reached Kashiari, where he captured Madaranzu. He received tribute from the cities round about, and then crossed the range into Nairi and halted at Shinigsha. Thence he went to Madara, which he captured and destroyed. Then he went to Tushkha and consecrated the palace there, receiving tribute from Nirdun. He destroyed sixty cities on the Kashiari range. Then he crossed the Tigris on rafts and reached Pitura, which he sacked. The same fate befell Kukunu and fifty cities in Dira. Then he went down to Arbaki where the inhabitants fled to Mount Matni. Great slaughter followed, and 250 strong cities in Nairi were destroyed. The people of Bît Zamani revolted against their governor, and Ashur-natsir-pal captured all the treasures of the place. So at the end of five years' reign Ashur-natsir-pal could boast that he had no rival from the Tigris to the Lebanon range and the Mediterranean Sea.

Kalah was now ready to receive him, and on his next expedition he started thence. He then crossed the Tigris and halted at Tabit; there he received much tribute and went on to the river Kharmesh and stopped at Magarisi; thence to the Habur and stopped at Shadikani and received tribute. Again he went on to Qatnu and received tribute from Shunaia. Thence to Dûr-katlime, then to Bîti-Khalupi, where he received tribute, and went to Sirku and received tribute. Then he went to Supri, then to Naqarabani, then to Khindanu close to a mountain on the Euphrates, then to Bît Shabaia, then to Ilat, then to Sûru, everywhere receiving tribute. Sûru, however, was dependent on the Kashshi, i.e. Babylonia, and its viceroy came out to join battle. He was defeated and Ashur-natsir-pal captured the city, fifty horses, and the troops of Nabû-apli-iddina, king of Karduniash, and his brother Zabdânu, and the Babylonian soothsayer who led their forces. This put fear into the hearts of the Babylonians and Chaldæans. He set up his image in Sûru.

When, however, Ashur-natsir-pal had returned to Kalah, he heard that Laqê, Khindânu, and Sukhi, had revolted and crossed the Euphrates. So again he left Kalah, crossed the Tigris, marched into the desert, and approached Sûru. He built ships of his own and marched up the Euphrates to the "narrows." Then he captured the cities in Laqê and ravaged up the Habur to Sibate in Sukhi. Then in his ships he crossed the Euphrates at Kharida. He met a large rising of the coalition and defeated them, captured Kipina, a city in Khindânu, and drove its king to Mount Bisuru. Slaying and plundering, Ashir-natsir-pal pursued the fugitives to Dummete and Asmu in Bît Adini. The king of Laqê, with many captives, was carried to Assyria. Ashur-natsir-pal now founded two cities on the Euphrates, one on each side, Kar-Ashur-natsir-pal and Nibarti-Ashur.

Again Ashur-natsir-pal left Kalah and marched into Bît-Adini to Kaprabi, which he took, and deported 2400 of its people to Kalah. Then he received tribute from Bît-Adini and Til-abnâ.

Once more Ashur-natsir-pal started from Kalah, crossed the Tigris, and took the road to Carchemish. He received tribute from Bît-Bakhiani, and reinforced by chariots, cavalry, and infantry, from thence went to Asalli and received tribute. Then he reached Bît-Adini and received more tribute and re-inforcements. Til-abnâ sent its tribute, thence he crossed the Euphrates and drew near to Carchemish, which was held by Sangara, king of the Hittites. Here again he received valuable presents and further reinforcements, and went on between the mountains of Munzigana and Khamurza towards Lebanon. He received tribute from Khazazi in Patini and pushed on across the Apri River. After a halt, he reached Kunulua, the capital of Patini, and received the sub-mission and tribute of its king. Also tribute from Iakhani came in. Then Ashur-natsir-pal crossed the Orontes and marched on between the mountain Iaraqi and Iaturi. He next halted at the river Sangura, then he marched between the mountains of Saratini and Duppâni. Again a city of Patini was taken and Lukutu plundered and garrisoned. Then he visited Lebanon and went on to the Mediterranean. He " washed his weapons " in the Great Sea. Here he received tribute from Tyre and Sidon, Byblos, Makhalata, Maisa, Kaisa, Amurru, and Arvad. He visited Amanus and cut down cedar trees and other valuable wood. Again he set up a statue of himself on Amanus.

In the next year he crossed the Tigris and went down to Qipani. Here he received tribute from

Khuzirina, from Salla, Ashsha, Commagene, and the districts round. Then he marched up the Euphrates, passed through Kubbu, and went into Ashsha and Kirkhi. He captured Umalia and Khiranu, in Adani. He then left Karania, and entered the pass of Amadani and went into Dirria. He wasted Amadani, Arqania, and annexed Mallânu. Then he entered Zamba, and plundering the district crossed the Sûa and was on the Tigris again. He ravaged all that district, received great spoil, took hostages, and appointed a governor. Then he went down to Barzanishtun and reached Damdamusa, which he stormed, and went on to Amedi, where he cut down the plantations. Next he entered the pass of Kashiari and reached Allabra. He stormed Uda and annexed it.

Everywhere, with wearisome repetition, Ashur-natsir-pal records the slaughter of thousands, thousands of captives, enormous spoil, and destruction of cities and lands. The details are far too numerous to repeat after him. He often turned aside to hunt and records great numbers of wild beasts slain. His annals come down to the eighteenth year of his reign. Apart from the awful picture of this terrible scourge of men, his narrative is of deep interest for the light it throws upon geography and, in the details of his spoils or tribute, upon the productions of the various districts. In

many points it is clear that he followed in the foot-
steps of the great Tiglath-pileser I., and we may
suspect some of his boasts of exaggeration. His
achievements were clearly the greatest of any
Assyrian monarch up to his day, and he left his son
a great heritage to maintain.

SHALMANESER III., B.C. 860.—The whole thirty-
five years of this king's reign were a protracted
military expedition. Shalmaneser, on his celebrated
Black Obelisk, narrates in brief sentences thirty-two
expeditions, and these are invaluable as annals to
arrange the events of the reign. Special features
of the history are commemorated at fuller length on
other monuments of his reign. We have better
information about this king than about any later
monarch until Sargon II. We are able to date his
achievements with unusual accuracy.

Early in his reign, Shalmaneser met with a good
excuse for interfering in Babylonia, B.C. 852. Nabû-
apal-iddin had cleared out the Aramæans, who had
made extensive inroads. He kept the peace with
Assyria and made alliance with Shalmaneser, but after
a prosperous reign of thirty-one years, his people
deposed him and put Marduk-nâdin-shum, his son,
on the throne. He had apparently set his son
Marduk-bêl-usâte in power over the Aramæans.
The latter led his forces against the new king of
Babylon, apparently to avenge his father, but also

to take the sceptre from his brother. Shalmaneser responded to Marduk-nâdin-shum's appeal for help, marched an army into Babylonia, defeated and killed Marduk-bêl-usâte, and made Marduk-nâdin-shum a vassal king. Then, as a sign of his supremacy, Shalmaneser visited in pomp the great temples of Babylon, Borsippa, and Kutha, making rich offerings to the gods. The new overlord proceeded to set Babylonian affairs in order. The Chaldæans had many city-states in Lower Babylonia, and were perpetually attempting to encroach upon Babylon. Shalmaneser attacked them, and after defeating all opposition, laid regular tribute upon them.

Shalmaneser took up the work of consolidating his father's conquests in Syria. Of course, some of the tributary states had rebelled. Bît-Adini, doubtless reinforced from the western states, took four expeditions to settle affairs, B.C. 859-856. The league of states was soon broken up, and Akhuni, king of Bît-Adini, fought on by himself for three years, but was finally taken prisoner to Asshur. Carchemish, Sama'al, and Patini submitted and sent tribute. Shalmaneser colonised his conquests, renamed and garrisoned the cities of Bît-Adini, and pushed on south-west into new fields. Here he had to reckon with Hamath, Damascus, and Israel. Khalman (Aleppo) was his advanced post. Hamath lay eighty miles south, Damascus one hundred miles farther,

BLACK OBELISK OF SHALMANESER III.

and Israel bordered the kingdom of Damascus. Israel then controlled Judah, Moab, and Edom. Damascus and Hamath were in alliance with the western city-states. There was incessant war between them as each in turn sought supremacy. Damascus had in the interests of Judah defeated Omri. But the Assyrian advance made them all unite for mutual protection. Irkhuleni of Hamath, Adad-idri of Damascus, and Ahab of Israel united with nine other people, Quê, Mutsri, Arvad, Usanate, Shiana, Arabia, Ammon, etc., met the Assyrian with an army of 4000 chariots, 2000 horsemen, 1000 camel corps, and 63,000 footmen, at Qarqar on the Orontes. The Assyrian claimed the victory, but could not follow up his advantage. His vassals in Mesopotamia rebelled, and in B.C. 850 Carchemish and Bît-Agusi were chastised. In B.C. 846 he attacked the allies with the whole militia of Assyria, putting an army of 120,000 men in the field; again he retired baffled, if victorious. Three year later, B.C. 843, he made an expedition to the Amanus successfully, but without disturbing the allies. Doubtless he was intriguing all the time, and in Damascus Adad-idri was deposed by Hazael. Ahab had fallen in battle with Damascus, and the house of Omri was exterminated by Jehu. Shalmaneser now marched west, and passing Khalman, Hamath, and Damascus, separated the allies. Hazael attacked the Assyrians on the east

of Mount Hermon. They defeated him and drove
him back to Damascus, but the city was too strong.
They ravaged the land down to the Hauran. Hamath
did not move. Tyre and Sidon sent tribute. Israel
also sent a rich tribute. Hazael was unsubdued.
Shalmaneser again attacked in B.C. 839, and again
received tribute, but could not conquer Damascus.
Shalmaneser then gave up the contest. Hazael
had been deserted by his allies, and soon took
vengeance on them. Israel became his vassal, and he
gradually became lord of all the south down to
Egypt.

Shalmaneser had to be content with North Syria,
and three campaigns where he subdued Quê (Cilicia)
and captured Tarsus fall in B.C. 840, 835, 834. Tabal
was reduced in B.C. 838, and Malatia in B.C. 837.
When Patini rebelled it was easily set in order by
the Tartan, B.C. 832. Thus Assyria commanded the
north-west route into Asia Minor.

The control of the upper Tigris was his and the
hinterland of Armenia had been made incapable of
harm, but the absence of Assyrian armies in the
west raised hopes of independence. Besides, a
new nation calling itself Khaldia, after its national
god Khaldis, but to be soon known to Assyria as
Urartu, was gathering strength. Ashur-natsir-pal
had come in contact with them, but did not fight
them. The first kings were Lutipris and Sarduris I.,

followed by Arame. The last named king succeeded in making a strong state. It reached along the north of the Taurus to Milid and occupied the east of Lake Van. It was disposed to acquire Assyrian culture, for it used Assyrian characters and language for its earliest inscriptions on stelæ, evidently close copies of Assyrian models. But its own native genius soon modified the form of writing to the characteristic Vannic, and wrote in the Vannic tongue. Shalmaneser evidently viewed the progress of Urartu with jealousy, for he sent an expedition to Khubushki, south-west of Lake Urmia, and thence attacked Urartu, B.C. 860. After his conquest of Bît Adini, he followed the river upwards and marched along the west of the Kashiari range up the Taurus. Here he merely wasted the country, as a safeguard, and attacked Urartu. He was thus able to penetrate to Arame's capital, Arzashku, and capture it. He came back through Gilzani, on the north-west shores of Urmia, where he met with the two-humped drome- dary, and into Khubushki and out again above Arbela. It was a march of close on a thousand miles. Another expedition from the sources of the Tigris fell in B.C. 845. In B.C. 853 a similar campaign took place under the Tartan. Arame was succeeded by Sarduris II., with whom the Tartan fought in B.C. 829, and then by Ishpuinis, with whom the Tartan in B.C. 819 crossed swords. It is evident that these

G

incessant little wars were fine training for the
troops of both Assyria and Urartu, but the victory
lay largely with Assyria. The restlessness of Urartu
stirred up other peoples, whom the Assyrian king
annexed.

The Mannai, south and west of Lake Urmia,
Mazamûa and Parsûa to the south, and the Madai
or Medes to the east, were brought under Assyrian
sway. These Medes and Persians may not yet have
been of the Indo-European race, but when those
people came into the same districts they took over
the names. The Persians had come first, and the
Madai were new-comers. They had rolled up and
confined the tribes welded into one as Urartu.
Their continued pressure led to Urartu's move to
the south. The Assyrians discovered that such incursions must be dammed back. But Shalmaneser,
at any rate, left Assyria in power round Lake
Urmia.

Shalmaneser wisely left much of his military work
to his generals, but he was far from idle at home.
He built extensively in Asshur, and especially at its
walls. In B.C. 834 he entirely rebuilt the whole city
wall, repairing damages due evidently to former
sieges which had effected three breaches. In the
statues of himself, set up in a recess of the Gurguri
gate at Asshur, we may see his portrait to-day. He
rebuilt the temple in B.C. 858.

Katî, king of Tabal, sent his daughter with a rich dowry to Shalmaneser at Asshur.

Shalmaneser III.'s own accounts go down to his thirty-first year, B.C. 829. This very year, when the Black Obelisk was finished, a rebellion broke out which split the empire in two. We only know of it from the short notice left by the next king, and the records of the *Eponym lists*. Shalmaneser's own son, Ashur-danin-apli, rebelled. How he managed to get so much of Assyria on his side and for so long we cannot now conjecture. Shalmaneser's favour to Babylon may be the clue. But while Shalmaneser was able to hold Kalah, most of the Assyrian chief cities -- Nineveh, Asshur, Arbela, the colonies at Amedi, Tîlabnâ, Khindanu held out for Ashur-danin-apli, whom we must therefore regard as king *de facto*. Shalmaneser died after four years of this divided rule, and his other son and legal successor, Shamshi-Adad, had to fight for his crown two years more.

SHAMSHI-ADAD VII., B.C. 823-811.—In consequence of the long civil war, Assyria naturally everywhere lost authority. Shamshi-Adad set out to reduce the north. Nairi had to be reclaimed, and then he traversed Assyria from Paddira, on the border of Nairi, to Kar-Shalmaneser, on the border of Carchemish; from Zaddi, in the Babylonian territory, to Enzi ; and from Aridi to Sukhi. But Shamshi-Adad succeeded in recovering the lost ground in all these regions.

His second campaign was conducted by the commander-in-chief of the army, and covered Nairi and northern districts. Here 511 cities were reduced to submission, paid tribute, and suffered punishment.

In his third campaign Shamshi-Adad crossed the Zaban, and went up Mount Silar again to Nairi. He received tribute from Khubushki, Sunbai, Mannai, Parsûa. Taurla and Mesu submitted, and he destroyed 500 cities in the district. Then he went to Gizilbunda, captured Kinaki, received tribute from Sasiashai and Karsibutai. Then he turned to the Medes, and after plundering their district he punished Araziash, and finished off by Kharkhar. The inscriptions teem with details of tribes and cities, kinglets and princes in Nairi and round to the borders of Elam. But the Assyrian was everywhere victorious, and reaped a rich harvest of spoil and captives.

In his fourth campaign he started for Karduniash, crossed the Zab, and passed the Zaban by Zaddi, killed three lions, and then went up Mount Ebikh and invested Mê-Turnat, which submitted. Then he crossed the Turnat and invested Karnê and 200 villages in its district. He then climbed Mount Ialman and invested Di'ibina, which submitted. Datebir, Izduia, on the Gananati, and 200 villages

STELE OF SHAMSHI-ADAD.

were reduced. A number held out desperately in Kiribti-abâni, which was taken later and razed to the ground. Then the people of Akkad attempted to stem the tide of success, holding Dûr-Papsukkal on an island in the stream. But it was without avail, and one by one 447 towns and villages fell into his hands. Shamshi-Adad claims to have slain 13,000 of the enemy and taken 3000 captives, and appropriated all the royal property which fell into his hands, while private property was given as loot to his soldiers. The Babylonian king, Marduk-balatsu-ikbi, summoned to his help the Chaldæans, Elam, Nairi and the Aramæans. Shamshi-Adad records a tremendous slaughter of the enemy. The last five years of his reign were taken up with five campaigns in Babylonia. He defeated Bau-akh-iddina, Marduk-balatsu-ikbi's successor, and carried him and his belongings to Assyria. He captured Dûr-ilu, Lakhiru, Gananati, Dûr-Papsukkal, Bît Ridûti, Mê-Turnat, cities mostly on the east side of Babylonia, and carried off the gods of Maliki. Then, as token of his supremacy, he offered sacrifice at Kutha, Babylon, and Borsippa. He advanced into Chaldæa and received tribute from its kings, and so Babylonia was once more at the feet of Assyria. The *Synchronous History* compiled in his son's reign gave the final boundary decisions, now unfortunately lost. A fragment of the treaty which he concluded

with Marduk-shum-iddin of Babylon is still preserved, but it does not appear to be very favourable
to Assyria. It probably dates from the time of the
civil war, when Shamshi-Adad may have been glad
of Babylonian support. Perhaps it was at this
time that he married his son to Sammuramat,
daughter of the Babylonian king.

ADAD-NIRARI IV., B.C. 810-782.—His own inscrip-
tions trace his genealogy back to Shalmaneser, and
assert his claim to descent from Bêl-kapkapu, who
was king before Sulili, *i.e.* Sumu-la-ilu, established
Babylonian rule over Assyria. He claims to have
conquered from Mount Siluna in the east, including
Ellipi, Kharkhar, Araziash, Mesu, Madai, Gizilbunda,
Munna, Parsua, Allabria, Abdadana, round by Nairi,
Andia, to the Great Sea in the west, and along the
Euphrates from the Hittites in the east to the Amurri,
Tyre, Sidon, Khumri (*i.e.* Israel), Edom and Palestine
again to the sea coast. He had, however, to make
an expedition to Damascus and besiege its king Mari'.
The Syrian king submitted, gave up an enormous
tribute, and became a vassal. The kings of the
Chaldæans also became vassals, and the king of
Assyria again offered in Babylon, Kutha and Borsippa.
He favoured Kalah as a residence, and built a temple
there for Nabû, god of wisdom, and the learning
which Adad-nirari fostered. His queen was Sammurammat, clearly a Babylonian princess. Her name

and the tradition of her great influence may lie
behind Herodotus (I. 184), who makes Semiramis
rule over Babylonia. The statue of Sammurammat still stands in Asshur.

The *Eponym lists* give the following entries of
expeditions :—B.C. 810 to Madai ; B.C. 809 to
Guzana ; B.C. 808 to Mannai ; B.C. 807 Mannai
again ; B.C. 806 to Arpad ; B.C. 805 to Khazazi ;
B.C. 804 to Ba'li ; B.C. 803 to the Sealand (Chaldæa ?),
a pestilence ; B.C. 802 to Khubushki ; B.C. 801
and 800 to Madai ; B.C. 799 to Lulumê ; B.C. 798
to Namri ; B.C. 797 to Mantsuate ; B.C. 796 to Dûr-ilu ;
B.C. 795 again ; B.C. 794 and 793 to Media ; B.C. 792
to Khubushki ; B.C. 791 to Itu'a ; B.C. 790 and 789
to Media ; B.C. 788, a festal year ; B.C. 787 to Media,
and the god Nabû entered his new temple ; B.C. 786
to Kish ; B.C. 785 to Khubushki, and the great god
Anu came to Dûr-ilu ; B.C. 784 to Khubushki ;
B.C. 783 to Itu'a and again in B.C. 782.

A little note of the position of affairs in this reign
is that Bêl-tartsi-an-ma, who set up a statue of Nabû
at Kalah for the life of Adad-nirari and Queen
Sammurammat, was viceroy of Kalah, of Amedi,
Sirgana, Temeni and Ialuna. His seal is still preserved at the Hague.

SHALMANESER IV., B.C. 781-772.—We have few
historical inscriptions of this reign. From the
Eponym list we learn that the war against the Itu'a, a

troublesome nomad folk on the borders of Babylonia, went on. In B.C. 781 to 778 expeditions to Urartu under Shamshi-ilu, the Tartan, were repeated against Argistis I. In B.C. 777 the Itu'a were again dealt with. In B.C. 776 Urartu once more. Then an expedition was made to the land of Erini. In B.C. 774 expeditions were sent to Urartu and Namri. In B.C. 773 and 772 the army operated against Damascus and Hadrach.

ASHUR-DÂN III., B.C. 771-763.—We are again forced to rely upon the *Eponym list*. In B.C. 771 an expedition went to Gananati, in B.C. 770 to Marad, in B.C. 769 to Itu'a. The army remained at home in B.C. 768. In the next year Gananati was again attacked. In B.C. 766 an expedition was sent to Media. In B.C. 765 Hadrach was dealt with. In B.C. 764 the army remained at home. The *Eponym Canon* here makes its most celebrated entry. There was a rebellion in Asshur, and in Sivan the sun was eclipsed. This note enables us to date events so far as recorded in the *Eponym Canon* with certainty from B.C. 911 to B.C. 640. But the Canon does not mention the fact established with certainty from other considerations that the rebellion led to the accession of Adad-nirari, son of Ashur-dân. Whether he actually reigned from B.C. 763 to B.C. 755, or whether possibly his father resumed the throne, cannot be ascertained.

ADAD-NIRARI V., B.C. 763-755.—This king made grants to the temples in Maganuba, and set there three priests whom he endowed, and of whom one survived to the first year of Sargon II. The *Eponym Canon* gives the following events for these years. In B.C. 762 there was still a rebellion in Asshur; in B.C. 761 there was rebellion in Arapkha, as also in B.C. 760. In B.C. 759 there was rebellion in Guzana and a pestilence; B.C. 758 saw an expedition to Guzana and peace in the land. The next two years the army remained at home. In B.C. 755 an expedition to Hadrach took place, and next year to Arpad. A return from Asshur took place. This marked a step in the reorganisation of the country, but what it implied is not clear. Next year, or this perhaps, Ashur-nirari came to the throne.

ASHUR-NIRARI IV., 753-746.—For four years his army remained at home, and the first foreign expeditions were to Namri in B.C. 749 and 748. The army remained at home in B.C. 747, the year when Nabonassar came to the throne in Babylon, an event evidently regarded there as the foundation of a new era. Next year there was a rebellion in Assyria and as its result Tiglath-pileser came to the throne. Ashur-nirari made a treaty with Mati-ilu of Agusi, of which a copy has been preserved. Mati-ilu acknowledged him as overlord and undertook to engage in no war without his permission. Bît Agusi, his kingdom, lay within the district, of which Haran was the capital.

TIGLATH-PILESER IV., B.C. 745-727.—On the 13th of Aiaru, in B.O. 745, Tiglath-pileser seated himself on the throne, and in Teshri he crossed the river obviously to lead out an expedition and assert himself as a conqueror. The first year saw an expedition to Namri. We know nothing of Tiglath-pileser's origin, but his reign shows him to have been well versed in military matters. We may assume that he owed his elevation to the discontented army, whose resentment at being kept at home five out of seven years must have been intense. He never lays claim to royal descent. When later he came to the throne in Babylon, he was known as Pûlu. It may have been his proper name, and Tiglath-pileser a name adopted by him in memory of the great conqueror.

His attitude to Babylon under Nabonassar and his two successors was friendly. So long as Babylon was content to remain peacefully under the protection of Assyria he had no need to move, and other things claimed his attention. Tiglath-pileser built himself a palace at Kalah, on the ruins of an old palace of Shalmaneser's. He adorned it with many fine sculptures and inscriptions which, however, suffered an evil fate. Esarhaddon used the slabs for his own palace, turning their faces to the wall, and cutting his own inscriptions on their backs. It is the more unfortunate since they were drawn up as Annals, and we have few chronologically arranged inscriptions of this reign. The *Eponym Canon* helps us to a great extent.

He started with a military tour through Babylonia. The Aramæan tribes on the lower Euphrates, up to the Tigris and Uknu, were a menace to the cities there. Dûr-Kurigalzu, Sippar, Pazita, the Kutî, and Itu'a, who had given his predecessors incessant trouble, the Rubu' and other Aramæans, were subdued. He built a city at Til-Kamri, and called it Kar-Ashur. He "smashed" Bît-Shilâni, captured Sarrabanu and made it a heap of ruins, impaling its king before its gates; he "thrashed" Bît-Amukkani, and broke down the resistance of the Pukudu (Pekod), the Ru'a, Litau and other Aramæans, and set fresh tribute on the chiefs of the Chaldæans. He offered his sacrifices in Nippur, Kutha, Sippar and Babylon.

Then he settled the restless Median districts and the states on the Elamite border, putting in viceroys and enacting tribute as far as the Bikni range.

Urartu was the only state of consequence which was now at enmity with Assyria; and Sarduris III. had made an alliance with Mati-ilu of Agusi. They had moved into Commagene, and annexed Kishtau. Urartu had got so far as invading Syrian lands, and in B.C. 743 a slaughter of the Urartai took place in Arpad. Sarduris had taken the title of king of Syria. Sulumal of Malatia and Tarkhulara of Gamgum had combined with him. Tiglath-pileser pursued the defeated army to the bridge of the Euphrates, and the war was transferred to the north. Both in Commagene and from Nairi Assyrian forces pressed on. In North Syria the kings Kustaspi of Commagene, Rezin of Damascus, Hirom of Tyre, Urikki of Quê, Pisiris of Carchemish, and Tarkhulara of Gamgum were reduced to their previous vassal condition. Tutammu of Unqi, in Patini, alone held out, and his capital, Kinalia, was stormed and the land made a province, where the Assyrian governor resided in Tutammu's new-built palace. This was apparently accomplished concurrently with the suppression of revolt in Nairi land. There, as of old, the Assyrian went plundering and destroying city after city, and the capture of Ullubu in B.C. 739 marked the re-establishment of Assyrian authority. Arpad was captured after three years' siege in B.C. 740. The resistance in North Syria ended with the capture of Kullani in B.C. 738 (Calno ?). Hamath was devastated and put under an Assyrian governor. Panammu of Sama'al and the northern Iaudi was acknowledged vassal king in North Syria. Menahem of Israel, and Zabibi, queen of Arabia, paid tribute.

In B.C. 735 Tiglath-pileser entered Urartu itself.

The capital now was Turushpa, near Lake Van. The citadel lay on a lofty rock in the lake. A large town spread on the shore. It was easy enough to take the town, but the citadel was invested in vain. Urartu was ravaged from end to end. In B.C. 734 Pekah of Israel had joined with Rezin of Damascus, Hanno of Gaza, and the Philistine states to attack Judah. Ahaz applied to Assyria for help. For three years Tiglath-pileser campaigned in Palestine. In B.C. 734 he attacked the south, freeing Judah from danger, and punished the Philistines. Hanno of Gaza fled to Mutsri. Pekah of Israel was deposed, and Hosea set up in his place. Damascus was invested two years, while the land was devastated. At this siege Panammu of Sama'al fought on the Assyrian side, and died in the campaign. Tiglath-pileser conducted the body with great pomp to his home, and set Bar-Requb, his son, on the throne. Tiglath-pileser finally took Damascus, and carried Rezin captive to Kir. Damascus became an Assyrian province. Samsi, queen of Arabia, withheld her tribute, but was followed up and defeated with great loss of her camels, and forced to accept an Assyrian resident at her court. The Sabæans sent tribute, and a governor over Mutsri was appointed. In B.C. 734 to 732 the kings of Ammon, Moab, Edom, and cities in Phoenicia appear in tribute lists. Tyre also paid tribute.

The authority of Assyria now extended from Cilicia to the Gulf of Aqaba, and woe betide any who should slight it. The king of Tabal did not attend to honour Tiglath-pileser's presence in Syria, and was promptly deposed. The king of Askelon, encouraged by Rezin's resistance, was perfunctory in his duties, but the fall of Damascus threw him into a fit of sickness, and he resigned his throne to his son, whom Tiglath-pileser acknowledged as his successor.

Ahaz of Judah was more politic and visited Tiglath-pileser at Damascus, and brought back to Jerusalem an Assyrian altar, which perhaps was intended to grace Tiglath-pileser's visit to Jerusalem.

Affairs in Babylonia had gone wrong after the death of Nabonassar in B.C. 734. He was succeeded by his son, who was soon put out of the way by one of his officers who became king as Nabû-shum-ukin. The Chaldæans at once seized the opportunity, and Ukinzêr, the chief of Bît Amukkani, turned the pretender off the throne, after two months' reign, in B.C. 732. On his return from the west, in B.C. 731, Tiglath-pileser took the matter up and marched into Babylonia, down the Tigris to Bît Amukkani. Ukinzêr was shut up in his capital, Sapia, while Tiglath-pileser cut down palm-trees and ravaged that and neighbouring lands. It was an exhausting enterprise, and Tiglath-pileser remained at home for a year, and then put out all his efforts in B.C. 729.

He was successful, Sapia was stormed, and **Ukinzêr** disappeared from the scene. Merodach-Baladan, **the** king of Bît Iakîn, offered tribute. Then in B.C. 729 and again in B.C. 728, Tiglath-pileser took the lands of Bêl and was legitimate king of Babylon.

SHALMANESER V., B.C. 727-722.—On the authority of some uncertain texts it has been conjectured that Shalmaneser V. was son of Tiglath-pileser IV. and already governor of Syria. No inscriptions of his have yet been discovered, and the *Eponym lists* give little information beyond that he remained at home in B.C. 726 and then made an expedition each of the next three years, but without stating whither they were directed. The *Babylonian Chronicle* mentions the destruction of Sabarain, which may have fallen in his first year. The intrigues of Seve of Mutsri, probably not Egypt, succeeded in inducing Hosea of Israel to refuse tribute, and Tyre did the same. Shalmaneser came in B.C. 725 to the West and overran the whole of Phœnicia. After making treaties and peace with all, Samaria was besieged, and the siege was probably left to a detachment of the army. Before it was over the throne passed to Sargon II., how or why we cannot say.

The *Babylonian Chronicle* says that Shalmaneser had ruled five years as king of Babylon and king of Assyria. In Babylon he was known as Ululai, probably from the month of his birth in Elul.

CHAPTER VI

THE SARGONIDS

SARGON II., B.C. 722-705. — Sargon II., or as he is called in his own inscriptions, " Sargon the later," came to the throne of Assyria in Tebet, B.C. 722. Like Shalmaneser he was not of royal descent. At any rate he does not name his ancestors, and he may have owed his power to the army. The situation called for a statesman and a warrior. In Palestine and Syria rebellion was in full swing, though the siege of Samaria was being carried on with vigour. Whether he himself brought it to an end or had to leave its completion to the generals on the spot, his annals place its close at the very beginning of the reign. He carried off 27,290 men and settled his captives in the district of Gozan, Halah, and in the Median hill country ; while he filled Samaria and Galilee with colonists from Kutha and other recently conquered lands. Israel became an Assyrian province with a merely titular king and an Assyrian Resident. It was not so crushed as to be unable to take part two years later in the rising of Ilu-bi'di of

Hamath, but after that it appears simply as a subject province.

Babylonia was Sargon's first care. Merodach-Baladan II. was in full possession of the throne in B.C. 721. To be legitimate ruler of Babylon Sargon was bound to take the land of Bêl on the 1st of Nisan B.C. 721. Merodach-Baladan was supported by Elam, whose king advanced upon the Assyrian border and occupied Dûr-ilu on the lower Tigris. Sargon, whose army was still engaged in Palestine, rapidly pushed down the east bank of the Tigris with what troops he could collect. The battle was indecisive, except that the Elamites retreated and Sargon was able to punish the Aramæans who had sided with Merodach-Baladan, but the latter was acknowledged king in Babylon, where Sargon left him alone for twelve years.

It looked to the Palestinian chiefs as if Sargon was not equal to the task of holding his empire together ; and Ilu-bi'di, who had raised himself to the throne of Hamath, in alliance with Arpad, Tsimirra, Damascus, and Samaria, strengthened by the Mutsri and Hanno of Gaza, and encouraged by Egypt, made a bold effort to act as independent. In B.C. 720 Sargon overwhelmed Ilu-bi'di at Qarqar, captured him and flayed him alive, then pushed southward and crushed Sibi, or So, the general of Piru of Mutsri at Raphia. Hanno was taken captive to Assyria. The

H

Arabs, Piru of Mutsri, Samsi of Aribi, and Itamara of Saba brought tribute. The effect was peace in Palestine for seven years, but in B.C. 715 Sargon made a raid into Arabia and again received tribute from the same princes. Egypt fell under Shabako, and was paralysed for the time. The Ethiopian monarch, however, pursued the same policy, and his agents succeeded in encouraging Azuri of Ashdod to revolt. The Assyrian governors deposed him and set his brother Akhimiti on the throne. The citizens in B.C. 711 overthrew their puppet king, and a Yemenite adventurer was made king. Sargon sent a detachment of his picked troops to the spot, and before his allies could rally to his support the pretender was expelled. He took refuge in Arabia where a chieftain of Meluhha (Amalek) took him prisoner and sent him to Assyria. Ashdod, Gath, and Ashdudimma were made a province, Judah, Edom, and Moab paid tribute, and for a time Palestine feared the gods of Assyria.

But Sargon's resources were most strained by his campaigns in the north. The Armenian kingdom of Urartu was feeling the pressure of encroaching peoples to its north and west, and Sarduris III. having died, his son, Rusas I., took up the policy of consolidating the north. He so far succeeded, that a coalition of the states from the Mediterranean to Lake Urmia joined issue with Sargon. From

B.C. 719 to B.C. 708, Urartu in the north, and Mita of Mushku in the west, harassed the provinces and vassal states of Assyria. Rusas intrigued with Zikirtu, Umildish, and Bît Daiukku, states which had been made subject to Iranzu of Mannai by Tiglath-pileser IV. Sargon exerted his authority and punished the rebels in B.C. 719. Iranzu was succeeded in B.C. 716 by Aza, who, being faithful to Assyria, was murdered, and Bagdatti of Umildish seized his throne. Sargon defeated him and flayed him alive. The rebels then raised Ullusunu, his brother, to the throne. He submitted after a weak struggle, and Sargon accepted him as king. In B.C. 715 Rusas induced Daiukku of Mannai to rebel against Ullusunu, and Sargon deported him to Asshur. The Medes were already pressing hard on the subject states, and Sargon had to send punitive expeditions among them, who received the submission of many chieftains bearing Persian names. The inevitable conflict with Rusas came in B.C. 714. The king of Zikirtu gave the occasion. Rusas supported him, but was utterly defeated, and fled to his mountain fastnesses. Then the land was ravaged from end to end, its chief cities captured, and large portions of it alienated to the king of Mannai. Sargon then turned south-east to Ellipi, on the border of Elam, west of Lake Van, and eastward to the Caspian, everywhere receiving tribute and submission. The

whole area was made into Assyrian provinces. The
new king of Urartu, Argistis II., held a feeble rule,
but while ever intriguing was easily kept in check.
Sennacherib, the king's son, as we know from his
correspondence with his father, kept actively in
touch with all movements in Armenia, where Argistis
II. soon had to meet the Gimirri, who renewed their
incursions. He suffered severely at their hands.

Mita of Mushku, secure in his mountain stronghold,
was able perpetually to stir up strife in Quê, Cilicia
to the south-west, Tabal and North Syria to the
south, Commagene to the south-east, and Milid to the
east. He himself saw the aggressive movements of
the Gimirri to his east above Urartu with alarm, and
judged the time ripe to secure a retreat south, or
west. In B.C. 718 Tabal had to face rebellion in its
province Sinukhtu, then next year Pisiris, king of
Carchemish, declined to pay tribute. Sargon
stormed the ancient metropolis, deported its people,
and colonised the district from Assyria. It was
henceforth an Assyrian province. Quê next was
invaded by Mita, who attacked the land and robbed
it of territory. For a while its king made friends
with Mita, but later was replaced by an Assyrian
governor, who led the forces of Quê against Mita.
In B.C. 713 a singular piece of treachery occurred,
the king of Tabal, son of the prince whom Tiglath-
pileser IV. had set on the throne and himself

married to an Assyrian princess, who had twice received large accessions of territory from Sargon, actually rebelled. He fell, and Tabal became an Assyrian province. Next year it was the turn of Milid to be punished for rebellion. Its king had invaded the province of Kammanu. The king and royal family, as well as the chief inhabitants, were deported, and the land colonised with the Suti. Fortresses were erected against Mushku and Urartu. Its territory was partly handed over to the faithful king of Commagene. In B.C. 711 Sargon took occasion, on the murder of the king of Gamgum by his son, who then seized the throne, to make it into a new Assyrian province. With all these examples before his eyes, in B.C. 709 Mita made his submission to Sargon, who had despatched the governor of Quê against him. The opposition in the north-west was at an end.

Yet no sooner was Sargon at grip with Merodach-Baladan in B.C. 709 than the hitherto faithful king of Commagene was seduced from his allegiance by Argistis. When Sargon emerged from his great struggle triumphant, Commagene was made a full province. The whole west and north was thus subject to Sargon. Even the seven kings of Cyprus sent gifts, and in return received the conqueror's stele to be set up in that island.

Sargon, once free of dangers in the rear, turned to

recover Babylonia. Merodach-Baladan had filled the land with his Chaldæan favourites and ousted the native Babylonian magnates from property and office. He had found the throne no bed of roses, for he had evidently been obliged to suppress many rebellions. He had carried off the gods of Ur and Erech and the leading men of those cities, as well as of Sippar, Nippur, Babylon and Borsippa, to his capital in the far south, where he held them hostages. The Aramæan tribes were independent on the Tigris ; the Suti played havoc on the west of the Euphrates and in North Babylona.

Sargon marched down the east of the Tigris and made the Aramæan states, of which the chief was Gambuli, into a new Assyrian province. Elam was invaded, and its king retreated to the mountains. Then Sargon attacked Bît Dakkuri, a Chaldæan state, and thus cut off Merodach-Baladan from his base. The Chaldæan effected a junction with Elam, but Shutur-nanhundi, the new king, was useless and would not move. Sargon had strongly entrenched his army in Bît Dakkuri, and Merodach-Baladan retreated to his capital, Bît Iakin. The priests of Borsippa and Babylon came in procession, with the chief citizens, and invited Sargon to enter Babylon, where he took the lands of Bêl and became lawful king of Babylon, B.C. 709. He next had to drive the Aramæans out of Sippar, but soon turned to complete his southern conquests. He laid siege to Bît Iakin, stormed it, laid waste the land, deported the people, and colonised it. Merodach-Baladan escaped to the south of Elam. Sargon restored the ancient landowners, released the imprisoned Babylonians, brought back the gods of Ur and Erech to their temples, worshipped at the ancient altars, and endowed the shrines with rich gifts. The king of Dilmun, an island far down the Persian gulf, sent tokens of homage.

The whole ancient Empire of Sargon of Akkad had been won back by his namesake. It was a glorious conquest of the world. With good reason do the details of its progress fill the monuments of the conqueror. He had recovered a dangerous setback, received almost at his accession, and added greatly to his domains. Never once had his courage failed him in his darkest days.

A significant proof of this is that in B.C. 713, when Rusas was still unsubdued, Tabal was in full rebellion and Palestine barely settled, he began to build himself a huge new city to be the capital of his empire, to be called after his own name, Dûr-Sharrukin, Sargon-burgh. It took seven years to build. It lay at the foot of the hills in the northeast corner of Assyria proper, where the Jebel Maglub looks out like a snow-clad pyramid to Nineveh and Kalah. It was a beautiful situation, but

was not much cultivated, being hilly and bare. It
was in the *rêbit* of Nineveh, and some think it was
the Rehoboth-'ir (*rêbit* of the city) named in Gen. 10.
An old city, Maganubba, whose temple had been
endowed by Adad-nirari IV., had to be taken in, and
Sargon showed his genial nature by the care with
which he presented the old holders with new and
enlarged properties in exchange for the land he
absorbed. There he laid out a most carefully
planned city, a rectangle with its sides more than
a mile in length. The walls were over 50 feet high,
with towers 15 feet higher. Eight gates led into
the enclosure, which was laid out with streets and
parks, and might house eighty thousand people. On
the north-west side the royal palace stood on a terrace
raised level with the top of the walls. It covered
an area of 25 acres. The rooms, courts, towers
and gardens numbered nearly two hundred. The
great gate from the city front opened into a central
square. To the right were the royal storehouses or
arsenals; to the left was the Harem; opposite the
gate, the royal apartments and court-rooms. Here
were displayed the magnificent sculptures or bas
reliefs exhibiting the king's campaigns; the door-
ways were flanked with winged bulls, and the walls
and archways adorned with enamelled tiles. Coloured
stucco and frescoes covered the walls of less important rooms. The art displayed in the finish of

the work, the justice of the masonry, the colouring of the tiles and frescoes, the modelling of the furniture, as well as in the forms and finish of the weapons, is truly wonderful. The colossal character of the whole design, its independence of precedent, its broad display, the lofty *zikkurat* or stage tower, with seven stories, each coloured heraldically in accordance with its proper planet, rising to the height of 140 feet above the plain, gave a vivid impression of the wealth, resourcefulness and power of Assyria and its master mind, Sargon II.

While this was his great achievement at home, he cared, if somewhat less, yet very carefully for many cities of his realm. He names most of them as benefiting by his generosity, but others also benefited. He inhabited the ancient capitals, and there raised new palaces, or splendidly restored the old.

Sargon boasts that he colonised and restored ancient ruined cities, caused fields to be planted, made barren tracts productive, and waste dry lands fit for grain crops by his reservoirs, dams, and canals. He filled the granaries with corn, protected the needy from want, the weak from oppression, cheapened necessities and sought new markets. He filled his new city with a population from all lands, and strove to educate them by learned teachers, who should make them of one language " to fear God and the king." He began that library which his great

grandson made so famous in Nineveh. His piety
was remarkable for its adherence to the astrological
system, while he sought to rule all his actions by
reference to the will of God as manifested in the
starry sky, and as interpreted to him by his augurs.
In an especial manner he was " a man of the star,"
and much of his power was due to the hold which
his Messianic pretensions had on his people.

He was the father of a considerable family, and
Sennacherib was clearly not the eldest, though
Crown Prince and Viceroy in Assyria during the
last few years of Sargon's reign. Exactly how he
met his death is not known, but a broken inscription
connects it with some defeat or massacre, and
Sennacherib seems to have considered it needful
to bemoan his father's sins and make reparation for
them. Perhaps in his eyes the erection of a rival
to the old capital, Asshur, was a crime, but he himself
was guilty of the same thing later.

SENNACHERIB, B.C. 705-680.—Sennacherib came to
the throne at the end of July B.C. 705. The task before
him was the consolidation of an empire won by conquest and statesmanship. There was no national co-
herence, though a common language bound Assyria
and Babylonia together. Naturally, outlying districts
sought to shake off the Assyrian yoke, but the ever
victorious army was able to furnish troops for punitive expeditions to enforce supremacy on the Kassites

SIX-SIDED PRISM OF SENNACHERIB.

in the south-east hills, and Ellipi on the borders of
Elam, B.C. 702, to subdue Tabal and Mount Nipur
in the north-west. The Ionians appear to have
invaded Cilicia, perhaps having made alliance with
Kirûa of Illubru, who caused the people of Khilaku
(Cilicia) to revolt. With the help of Ingirâ and
Tarsus, Kirûa closed the Cilician road from Quê
to the Cilician gates. Sennacherib reinforced the
governor of Quê with picked troops, who cleared the
passes with great loss, but then captured Ingirâ and
Tarsus. In effecting the latter, Sennacherib appears
to have fought a naval battle with the Ionians. He
rebuilt Tarsus on the model of Babylon, probably
making the Cydnus play the same part for that city
as the Euphrates did for the latter. The erection of
an Athenian temple, ascribed to Sennacherib by
Abydenus, opens up an interesting question as to the
influence of Assyrian architecture on early Greek
forms, by way of the Ionians, who were deported in
large numbers to Assyria, and must have worked
on the palaces at Nineveh. Whether they in-
fluenced later Assyrian art is doubtful, but some of
the metal and ivory work shows Greek style. This
has usually been ascribed to the Phœnician commercial intercourse, but Cilicia may have been the
intermediary, and Hittite civilisation may be the
parent of much, both in Assyria and Asia Minor.
The expedition to Tarsus took place in B.C. 698, but

Sennacherib held it for some time. Three years later the expedition to Tabal occurred and dealt with restless mountaineers, with whom Tarsus does not seem to have combined.

Sennacherib's generals and governors kept the provinces in order, supported by the Assyrian military colonists and garrisons. The countries beyond the frontier were either too strong to attack or offered no special inducement. Of course Egypt kept on intriguing in Palestine, and Babylonia was a continual source of trouble. Babylon itself could make no claim to uphold an empire, but was coveted by many claimants. It was the fountain-head of civilisation, religion, and commercial activity, with fine traditions but devoid of warlike force. The Aramæans and Chaldæans ever sought to seize it. Sargon seems to have placed a brother of Sennacherib there as governor, who was murdered, and a Babylonian pretender, Marduk-zâkir-shum, came to the throne. Merodach-Baladan soon displaced him in B.C. 704. He strengthened himself by alliance with Elam and the Aramæans. Sennacherib defeated him at Kish and drove him out after nine months' rule. The Assyrian captured Babylon, seized the treasures of Merodach-Baladan, expelled the Chaldæans and Aramæans from Babylonia, and laid waste Chaldæa. On his return with two hundred and eight thousand captives, chiefly Aramæans,

Sennacherib raised Bêl-ibni, a scion of the old Babylonian royal house, reared at his own court to be king at Babylon, keeping South Babylonia under his own governors, garrisoned from Assyria.

Merodach-Baladan had laid his plans well. He had sent his embassies to Tyre, which had risen to considerable importance and power over Phœnicia. under its king, Luli. Hezekiah had come to the throne in Judah and was ready to listen to the ambassadors who succeeded in stirring up Ammon, Edom, Moab, and the Arab kingdoms. Padi of Ekron alone remained faithful to Assyria, but his people deposed him and sent him in chains to Hezekiah. The whole of Palestine, backed by Egypt, was in rebellion. Sennacherib, early in B.C. 707, marched to the Mediterranean, and the Phœnician cities submitted. Luli fled to Cyprus, though Tyre was not taken. Sennacherib appointed Itobaal as king of Sidon to act as check on Tyre, giving him the whole Phœnician land territory. Leaving his troops and his new subjects to make an attack on Tyre by sea, he passed down the west to Askelon. This he captured, and carried off Zidqa, its king. The allies met him at Eltekeh with a great army lead by Ethiopian, Egyptian, and Mutsri generals. This was merely a raiding mob, easily defeated. Eltekeh and Timnath were pillaged, and Ekron surrendered. The coast was cleared, and Hezekiah

could be reckoned with. Sennacherib systematically
reduced the land of Judah, capturing forty-six strong-
walled cities and a large number of smaller towns.
He deported 200,150 people and immense spoil.
Hezekiah was shut up in Jerusalem " like a bird in a
cage " and strictly invested. The territory was
assigned to Mitinti, king of Ashdod ; Padi, king of
Ekron ; and Tsilli-Bêl, king of Gaza. Hezekiah
asked for terms, and released Padi, paid an enormous
tribute as arrears, fine, and gave hostages surrender-
ing his allies from Arabia who had helped to garrison
Jerusalem. Thirty talents of gold, eight hundred
talents of silver, precious stones, couches and
thrones of ivory, costly furniture, his daughters,
palace women, male and female musicians, were sent
after Sennacherib to Nineveh. On the walls of his
palace Sennacherib had himself represented as
sitting in state outside Lachish, and having the
tribute of that city brought to him.

There seems to be little doubt that, as Esarhaddon
relates, and as some fragments of later inscriptions
tell us, Sennacherib made another expedition to
Arabia after B.C. 689, when his last great inscription
ends, and as a faithful ally Hezekiah ought then to
have furnished assistance and attended the king in
person. This he seems not to have done, and as a
consequence Jerusalem may have suffered a second
siege. At that time Sennacherib may have suffered

the terrible disaster described in 2 Kings xix., and narrated in other terms by Herodotus (II. 141). Until further evidence from contemporary monuments is available, it seems impossible to reconcile the Biblical accounts with Sennacherib's own story, or to date the second siege. The Biblical story, and all existing indications, point to the close of his reign, but from Assyrian sources we know nothing with certainty later than B.C. 691. Sennacherib's own accounts are engrossed again with Babylonia.

Bêl-ibni had not remained faithful. Perhaps he saw in Sennacherib's absence in the west a favourable chance. Merodach-Baladan took the field again with Elamite support. Marduk-ushezib was now the leader of the Chaldæans, but Sennacherib, in B.C. 500, entered Babylon, took Bêl-ibni and his supporters captive to Assyria, and drove back the Chaldæans to their swamps. Their capital, Bît-Iakîn, was besieged, but again Merodach-Badalan escaped with his gods to South Elam and there seems to have died soon after. Sennacherib now set his own son, Ashur-nâdin-shum, on the throne of Babylon, B.C. 699.

The Chaldæans had in great numbers emigrated to the coast of Elam and settled there. Thence they perpetually harassed Lower Babylonia. In B.C. 694 Sennacherib had matured a daring plan to exterminate this nest of pirates. He had built a navy on the Tigris, at Nineveh and other cities, probably

with the aid of his Phœnician and Cyprian captives;
and assembled it gradually at Opis. Thence he
floated it down the great canal into the Euphrates.
With great pomp was this new undertaking celebrated, when Assyrians for the first and last time
went to sea. With these ships, Sennacherib sent
over a detachment of his army, which destroyed
the Chaldæan sea-coast towns and brought back
their people captive to Babylonia.

Sennacherib had violated Elamite territory, and
his absence in the south suggested to Khallushu, king
of Elam, the opening for a counter-stroke. He
entered Babylonia, stormed Sippara, and massacred
its people, captured Ashur-nâdin-shum and carried
him to Elam, whence he never returned. Doubtless
this was facilitated by a native faction in Babylon,
for he set a native prince, Nergal-ushezib, on the
throne, B.C. 694-3. Content with this, he left Nergal-
ushezib to proceed south and take Sennacherib in
the rear. He succeeded in taking Nippur, but was
defeated by the Assyrian army soon after and taken
prisoner to Nineveh. His supporter fell victim to
a faction in his own land. Sennacherib attacked
the next king of Elam, Kudurnanhundi, in his own
land later. Babylon, deserted by and bereft of its
new king, was now seized by the Chaldæan, Mushezib-
Marduk, B.C. 692-89. The Babylonians accepted
him in the vain hope of resisting Sennacherib, who

was reckoning with Elam. After **nine months** Kudurnanhundi was murdered and Umman-men**â**nu made king. Mushezib-Marduk tried to buy his support with the treasures of Esagila, the great temple of Babylon. Sennacherib met the allies, who blackened the plain like a swarm of locusts, at Khalule, B.C. 691. He won a doubtful victory. Doubtless the greater part of his army was occupied elsewhere. Neither side moved for a time, but in B.C. 689 Umman-menânu was not inclined to help. Sennacherib captured Mushezib-Marduk and sent him to Nineveh. He now took vengeance for the murders of his brother and son. It may be that he also meant to secure for Nineveh an unrivalled supremacy in power. He razed Babylon to the ground, levelled not only fortifications and walls, but temples and palaces. The images of Adad and Shala, deities of the Assyrian city of Ekallâte, which Marduk-nâdin-akhi had carried off in the eleventh (?) century to Babylon, were now restored to their shrines. The seal of Shagaraktishuriash which Tukulti-Ninip I. had taken as spoil to Asshur, and had been brought back to Babylon, Sennacherib again took to Assyria. To complete its ruin the Arakhtu canal was destroyed and its waters turned over the city. Sennacherib henceforth ruled Babylonia by governors as an Assyrian province. There is good reason to think that Esarhaddon was

I

the governor in B.C. 680, and began to restore the city.

Ashur-nâdin-shum, doubtless, was heir to the throne, but after B.C. 694 another son, Ardi-Belit, was Crown Prince. Sennacherib built a palace for another son, Ashur-munik, in Tarbisi. But Esarhaddon was destined for the succession. Yet another son, Ashur-shar-etir, appears in a letter addressed to him by an Assyrian notable, who recognises him as king. Perhaps he was the son whose name appears as Sharezer in the Biblical account of Sennacherib's murder (2 Kings xix. 36). Who was meant by Adrammelech we have yet to discover. Contemporary sources only speak of one son, and do not name him. There is some reason to suppose that he was murdered in Babylon itself.

Sennacherib's name is indelibly associated with Nineveh, which owes its fame as a city, and chief representative of Assyria in the eyes of the later historians, to his choice of it. He found it an ancient city indeed, mentioned as long ago as Hammurabi, but sadly sunk in importance and subject to floods. The small river Choser, which comes down from the foot of Jebel Maglub and now runs directly through the ruins of Nineveh, washing the foot of the Kouyunjik mound, had in Sennacherib's time washed away the tombs of the kings, his ancestors. Sennacherib diverted it right and

left to pass along a deep moat at the base of the city
walls. The city was made into an irregular rectangle,
the western wall of which ran along the east Tigris
bank from north-west to south-east for two miles
and a half, its northern wall ran perpendicular to
this over a mile, while the eastern wall after
running parallel with the western for a mile bent
nearly south to meet after another two miles the
southern wall running almost due east, and half a
mile long. Protected by these lofty and massive
walls, on three sides by broad and deep moats, on
the river front by the Tigris itself, and reinforced by
powerful ramparts, walls and moats, across all
available approaches, it was impregnable for the
armies of that day. Probably an accidental flood
burst the dams and emptied the moats when the
Medes breached the walls at the north-east corner
by the Khorsabad gate. The road to the north-
west lay through difficult country, easily held ; the
road to Arbela on the east, the king's highway and
procession street for the triumphant armies of
Assyria, was too strongly fortified to be forced. The
road to the south-east to Babylonia and the south
was through a hill pass that could hardly be opened
except for light armed troops. We are told by
Diodorus that the walls were 100 feet high, never less
than 50 feet wide, at their base they were over 100
feet thick by the gates. Sennacherib found its

inhabitants dependent upon rainfall for water to drink, as the Choser is full of bitter salts and, moreover, drained many villages in its course. So he turned eighteen mountain streams into an aquaduct and led a supply into the ponds and tanks within the city. The great mounds of Kouyunjik and Nebi Yunus, close on the western wall, now parted by the Choser and largely built up artificially, served as platforms for the great palaces of Sennacherib, Esarhaddon and Ashur-bânipal. Sennacherib's palace, so far as accounts of explorations have been given, has only partly been excavated, yet seventy-one rooms have been examined, and it is thought to have been the finest ever built by the Assyrian kings. His great arsenal lay on the mound of Nebi Yunus.

The sculptures which adorned his rooms are among the finest productions of antiquity for variety of subject, accuracy of portraiture, simplicity and breadth of composition. The background is filled in most appropriately with details calculated to enhance the subject, and shows a most unexpected advance in the treatment of landscape.

Beside his creation of Nineveh he built extensively at Kalah, and at Asshur erected a palace for his son, Ashur-ilu-muballitsu.

Under this king a great advance in literary power manifests itself. The clear, pointed, but dry annals are enlivened by many little touches of humour, and a real gift for writing prose is developed. **For pure** dramatic power and vivid word painting **the de-** scription of the battle of Khalule would be difficult to surpass in any early literature. The collection **of** great works to form a library went on actively **at** Kalah, and a good foundation was being laid for Ashur-banipal's great library at Nineveh, many of the works in which were executed at this time. Sennacherib's correspondence with his father, Sargon, marks an advance in the art of letter-writing, which recalls the best models of the First Babylonian Dynasty.

In his building inscriptions he boasts of his method of casting bronze. He reintroduced the *shâdûf* for raising water from pools into the canals. He made a Hittite portico to his palace, and sent far and wide for foreign plants and trees to stock his gardens. Most prized by him were '' the trees that bear wool,'' from which the Assyrians sheared cotton for weaving garments. His description of the plant is precisely similar to that of Herodotus (iii. 106).

ESARHADDON, B.C. 680-668.—Sennacherib was murdered on the 20th of Tebet, early in January, and the rebellion was suppressed by Esarhaddon by the 2nd of Adar, the middle of February. He was crowned king on the 18th. His '' broken **Prism** '' preserves part of his account of the opening events of his reign. Giving command to his troops to reach the scene as rapidly as possible, he drove

post haste,. from Babylon apparently, to Nineveh.
" The furious cold of Shebat I did not fear." The
enemy had retreated north to Khanigalbat and overcame his advance guard, but as his main body
advanced the Assyrian troops came over to his side.
The murderers and their supporters fled to Armenia,
and Esarhaddon was proclaimed king, B.C. 681.

We do not possess his annals in the form in which
the kings loved to draw up the history of their reigns,
usually after they had borne the brunt of their wars,
and were at peace. He did not reign long enough to
see such an end. There is consequently some un-
certainty about the dates of his reign. He has left
many long inscriptions of the more picturesque sort,
and they are largely meant to commemorate his
buildings. He founded no new city, but restored
many. Alongside Sennacherib's arsenal he built a
palace which has hardly been touched by the
excavator. At Kalah, however, Layard laid bare
much of his palace in the south-west corner of
the mound. It was clearly left unfinished, piles
of slabs from the palace of Tiglath-pileser IV. lay
ready for being recut for his new building. He
restored the tunnel which brought water from the
upper course of the Zab to Kalah. He rebuilt the
temple of Ashur at Nineveh, and the temples at
Erech, Sippar, Dûr-ilu, Borsippa were restored by him.

Above all he reconstructed Babylon. It had

HEADS OF ENEMIES BROUGHT TO SENNACHERIB.

lain waste ten years when he gave orders to reinhabit
it. The population had naturally drifted back.
Such a site, with its traditions and its position
as centre of commerce, could not be kept unin-
habited except by force. The work of restoration
was completed in three years, B.C. 680-678. The
Chaldæans of Bît Dakkuri who had seized the
empty estates were expelled, and the ancient owners
reinstated. What induced him to revive such a
potent rival to his own capital is not easy to divine.
" Marduk had in his anger permitted destruction,
now in mercy turned back his face to favour his
beloved city." So Esarhaddon publicly describes
the reason why he reversed his father's policy.
His mother, Naqia, who governed the empire for
him when absent on his warlike expeditions, may
have been a Babylonian princess ; or he may have
grown attached to the place while governor there,
and seen in it the bulwark of his throne in the future.

A son of Merodach-Baladan, Nabû-zêr-napishti-
lishir, besieged Ur. The Assyrian governor of the
south raised the siege, and the Chaldæan fled to
Elam. There Umman-menânu had been succeeded
by Khumma-khaldash I., and he by a second king
of the same name. This king put the fugitive to
death. Another son of Merodach-Baladan, who had
shared his flight, now threw himself on Esarhaddon's
mercy, who at once made him vassal king of Chaldæa,

securing the peace of the south and an ally against Elam. Thus shut out from the south the Elamites raided Sippar in B.C. 674, while Esarhaddon was away in the west, and carried off the gods of Agade. They were repulsed by the Assyrian governors, and the ill success of the expedition cost the Elamite king his throne. He died the same year, and was succeeded by his brother, Urtagu, who returned the gods of Agade and remained at peace with Assyria. He had enough to do at home to keep back the Medes and Persians.

These half nomad folk were being pressed by new hordes from the north. The Gimirri had been just kept at bay by Urartu, and the Mannai, with Assyrian support, held Urartu in check. But a fresh wave split into two divisions. One went west into Asia Minor and was deflected into Phrygia, after, under Teushpa and Tugdamme (Lygdamis), having met Assyrian troops in Milid and Tabal. This was in B.C. 678. But the eastern branch was more successful. Repulsed from Armenia, they fell upon the Mannai. Driven off with difficulty they either conquered or amalgamated with the Medes. Then under the lead of Kashtarit, lord of Karkashi, the Gimirri, Medes and Mannai together threatened Assyria. Esarhaddon's policy staved off the invasion. Bartatua, chief of one branch, married an Assyrian princess ; some of the Medes made peace.

Expeditions against the Mannai and Ishpaka of Ashguza were successful, and every effort was made to play off one people against another. Urartu had suffered, for Esarhaddon, when he recovered the land of Shupria from the Gimirri, set free the imprisoned Urartreans, and Urartu allied itself with Assyria. The troubles ceased in B.C. 673, but it was only for a while.

In the west, Esarhaddon had more to do, and did it splendidly. Sidon had been fostered by Sennacherib as a check on Tyre. Itobaal was succeeded by Abdi-milkutti, who, in B.C. 678 withheld his tribute, relying upon the support of Sanduarri, a Cilician prince. Esarhaddon, in B.C. 676, reduced him to order ; he fled, but a few years later was caught, along with his ally, and both beheaded. Sidon was utterly destroyed, and an immense booty carried to Assyria. A new city was erected near by and called Kar-Esarhaddon, and Phœnicia made an Assyrian province. Ba'al of Tyre appears as a vassal king, and along with the kings of Cyprus helped to erect the new city, and contributed liberally to the building of Esarhaddon's palace at Nineveh. The list of vassals throws great light on the history of the west at this time : " Ba'al of Tyre, Manasseh of Judah, Qaushgabri of Edom, Musuri of Moab, Tsillu-Bêl of Gaza, Mitinti of Askelon, Ikausu of Ekron, Milkiashapa of Byblos, Matanba'al of Arvad,

Abiba'al of Samsimuruna, Budu-il of Ammon,
Akhimilki of Ashdod, the twelve kings of the sea-
coast; Ekishtura of Edial, Pilagura of Kitrusi,
Kisu of Sillua, Ituandar of Paphos, Eresu of Sillu,
Damasu of Kuri, Atmesu of Tamesu, Damusi of
Qarti-khadashti, Unasagusu of Sidir, Butsusu of
Nure, ten kings of Cyprus ' in the midst of the sea,'
in all twenty-two kings of the land of Khatti.''

Egypt always lay behind every rising in the west.
Esarhaddon now set to work to reduce it to in-
offensiveness. Sennacherib doubtless had planned
as much when he was besieging Jerusalem and raided
Arabia. Hazael of Arabia on that occasion had to
see his gods carried off. Now Esarhaddon sought
to have him on his side, and returned the gods.
Jailu had now succeeded to the throne and was well
disposed. Esarhaddon next felt for an opening in
the frontier. He first operated against the districts
Hazu and Bazu in south-west Arabia to secure his
flank. In B.C. 674 the Egyptian border was crossed,
but next year the Assyrian army was driven out.
Probably this reverse made Tyre venture to rebel.
Esarhaddon spent two years in making more extensive preparation, and after detaching forces to
screen off Ba'al of Tyre, the resistless Assyrian army
penetrated Egypt in earnest. Memphis was stormed
and sacked. The Crown Prince, Ushana-khuru, and
other royal princes, immense spoil and numerous

captives were taken to Assyria. Ethiopia was " rooted out " from Egypt. Esarhaddon appointed kings, governors, viceroys, officials of all sorts, and imposed regular tribute. He also provided an efficient system of posts and spies so that nothing could take place without his knowledge.

Esarhaddon on his return set up his stele at Sama'al where, a colossal figure, he appears holding in his hand a cord attached to rings in the lips of the two lesser figures, evidently Taharqa of Egypt and Ba'al of Tyre. A very similar image and inscription appear on the rocks at Nahr-el-Kelb by the side of the memorials of the proud Egyptian conquerors of earlier days. Esarhaddon was the first of the Sargonids to call himself " king of the kings of Egypt," and " king of Egypt and Cush."

He could not expect to be long left in this proud position. Taharqa next year was again in Egypt. Esarhaddon set out to face him in B.C. 668, but died on the march at the end of October. He had evidently doubted his power to return and made exact arrangements for the succession to the throne. At the feast of Gula, end of April, B.C. 668, he proclaimed Ashur-bânipal, his eldest son, king of Assyria, and Shamash-shum-ukin, king of Babylon. Other sons he appointed priests at Haran and elsewhere. A later writer states that in B.C. 669 Esarhaddon had to remain in Assyria and put many nobles to death.

The old Assyrian aristocracy probably resented his patronage of Babylon.

Esarhaddon adopted a remarkable new method of securing allegiance. He believed in the reality of gratitude, and repeatedly showed mercy to opponents, trusting them to remain his friends. He did not entirely break with the cruel traditions of the past, and his treatment of Sidon was savage. But his energy, personal courage, his statesmanship, were of a high order.

ASHUR-BÂNIPAL, B.C. 668-626.—Immediately upon the news of Esarhaddon's death, the Queen Mother, Naqia, with Ashur-bânipal, Shamash-shum-ukin and the great nobles of the realm, proclaimed Ashur-bânipal's accession to the throne, and he proceeded at once to carry out his father's plans. Esarhaddon's death was not allowed to postpone the expedition to Egypt. At once the rightful homage and congratulatory gifts were demanded and received, and the usual contribution of troops exacted from the vassal kings. Ashur-bânipal's list only records two changes of rulers, Iakinlu of Arvad had replaced Matan-ba'al, and Amminadbi now ruled in Ammon. Manasseh of Judah was still an obedient vassal, and Ba'al of Tyre did not fail. Taharqa had already reached Memphis and his army came out to meet the Assyrian troops. Beaten at first, he retreated to Thebes, and the province resumed its normal state.

Soon the Egyptian princes, Necho, Sharruludari and Paqruru, were found intriguing with Taharqa, but the Assyrian governor captured the two former and sent them to Nineveh. Ashur-bânipal pardoned Necho and made him king of all Egypt, supported by Assyrian garrisons. Taharqa left him in peace and died B.C. 666. His successor, Tanutamon, did not cause trouble for three years. Then he marched north. Necho and his Assyrian troops could not resist him. Necho was slain, and Psammetichus, his son, was expelled. Then in B.C. 661 Ashur-bânipal drove back the invader into Ethiopia, where he stayed, giving up the contest. Now the Assyrians captured Thebes and plundered it, carrying great spoil to Assyria. Egypt remained an Assyrian province. After the war in Elam, Ashur-bânipal deported colonists from Kirbit to Egypt. Psammetichus was reinstated as king with Assyrian support.

Thus to hold supremacy in Egypt, the west must have been well under control. Ba'al of Tyre, never faithful except by compulsion, was finally shut up in his island fastness, so strictly that famine forced him to submit. He sent his son as hostage, his own daughter and his brother's daughters, for the king's harem, with many costly presents. Ashur-bânipal sent back his son and accepted the women and the presents. Iakinlu of Arvad also sent his daughter, as did Mukallu of Tabal, and Sandasarme, a prince of

Cilicia. In the case of Arvad, this did not appease the king's wrath, for he deposed the faithless Iakinlu and set Aziba'al, his son, in his place. The fear of the Gimirri doubtless induced the north-western kings to seek Ashur-bânipal's favour. At any rate, Ashur-bânipal gives that as the motive which moved Gyges, king of Lydia, to ask for help. He was already consolidating his power, by the aid of Carian mercenaries. The Gimirri, however, became such a menace that events in Cilicia, Tabal, and Egypt having shown him what Assyria could do, he very naturally proposed to make alliance. Before he could make any use of the somewhat cool friendship Ashur-bânipal could offer, Gyges was able to manage his own affairs, and he did not send tribute. It greatly pleased the Assyrian monarch to be so courted.

Urtagu of Elam, in B.C. 665, was induced to make alliance with the Aramæans and Chaldæans, to raid Akkad and besiege Babylon. Doubtless the war party in Elam had pushed him on, for his want of success, when Ashur-bânipal drove him off, led to his death. He was succeeded by his brother, Teumman, who proceeded to put all the members of the seed royal to death. Sixty of them escaped to Assyria, and Teumman demanded their surrender. When Ashur-bânipal refused, another Elamite invasion followed. The Assyrian army checked the

Elamites at Dûr-ilu, and advanced to Susa. A decisive battle at Tulliz, on the Ulâ river, resulted in the overwhelming defeat of Elam. Teumman and his son were killed; the army decimated. It was the end of the Elamite sovereignty. The Assyrian conqueror made Khumbanigash, son of Urtagu, king in Elam, and his son, Tammaritu, king of Khidalu, an important province. Ashur-bânipal meant to prevent united action.

B.C. 660 was marked by the punishment of the Gambuli, whose rebellion had given Elam a free hand. Elam, like Babylon and Sidon before it, was reduced to utter helplessness. It was not without severe strain on Assyrian resources. Shamash-shum-ukin, whom Ashur-bânipal, in accordance with Esarhaddon's plan, set on the throne of Babylon, now made a bid for independence. He, like Merodach-Baladan before him, sent agents to provoke rebellion on the part of vassal states ; and the temple treasuries were opened to buy alliances. The plot embraced South Babylonia, Syria and Palestine, Arabia, even Egypt and Lybia. Elam, Arabia, the Aramæans and Chaldæans were won over. The garrisons in the south were tampered with, and the governor of Ur sent word to the governor of Erech, who duly reported it to Ashur-bânipal that Shamash-shum-ukin was fomenting rebellion.

In B.C. 652, Shamash-shum-ukin took overt measures. He closed the gates of his fortresses and forbade his brother to sacrifice in the Babylonian cities. It was a direct challenge. His allies at once besieged and took Ur and Erech. Elam marched an army into Babylonia. Whether instigated by Ashur-bânipal or not, Tammaritu deposed Khumbanigash, but carried on the war. He in turn was slain by Indabigash, B.C. 650, who withdrew the army from Babylonia. Ashur-bânipal had already besieged Sippar, Kutha, and Babylon itself. The south was soon reduced to order, Nabû-bêl-shûmâte, a grandson of Merodach-Baladan, and his Chaldæans, being driven into Elam. Finally, after a nominal reign of twenty years, Shamash-shum-ukin seems to have burnt himself in his palace. Babylon was reduced to the direst want by a three years' siege, and opened its gates. Ashur-bânipal was once more master of Babylon and took a bloody vengeance on all who had shared in the conspiracy. He himself, henceforth, ruled Babylon, as King Kandalanu, from B.C. 647 to his death.

Once more able to take the aggressive, Ashur-bânipal dealt with Elam. He demanded the surrender of Nabû-bêl-shûmâte, who was a traitor of the deepest dye. He had not only broken his oath of allegiance, by which he had saved his life, not only invaded a friendly country and abetted, doubtless for his own ends, a treacherous brother, but he had carried away Assyrian captives. Indabigash, as in honour bound, refused to give him up, and an Assyrian army was launched against him. A palace intrigue led to the murder of Indabigash, and Khumbakhaldash III. then reigned. He could not face the invaders, and the Elamites set Tammaritu, who had escaped and made peace with Assyria, in his place. He sought to effect by treachery what he could not compass by force, and tried to murder the Assyrian garrisons in Elam. His plot was betrayed, and he was imprisoned. Khumbakhaldash III. once more took the lead and gave battle to the maddened Assyrians. They swept all before them, devastated the country, besieged and sacked Susa (B.C. 644). Ashur-bânipal records the destruction of palaces and temples, indignities to royal tombs and images of the gods, the vengeance of age-long resentment of woes inflicted upon Babylonia. With pride he narrates the restoration of the statue of Nanâ of Erech, carried off by Elamites 1635 years before.

Once more Ashur-bânipal demanded the surrender of Nabû-bêl-shûmâte, who, however, saved the Elamite's face by taking his own life. Khumba-khaldash himself, with his rival pretender to the throne, Pae, fell into the hands of the invaders. So Elam disappeared from the scene, B.C. 640, as a

K

rival to Assyria. To so wretched a state was it reduced that Ashur-bânipal seems to have made no attempt to rule it, and the Medes had no opposition to their annexation of it.

The Arabian states next felt the weight of Ashur-bânipal's resentment. Jailu, whom Esarhaddon had made a king, had fallen into Shamash-shum-ukin's toils. He sent assistance in the great rebellion, and also raided Syria and Palestine. He met with little success, and the Assyrian generals soon repulsed him and drove him from his kingdom, and finally he surrendered. The leadership then fell on Waite, who also gave trouble, allying himself with the Kedarenes and Nabatæans, and invading the western provinces. Ashur-bânipal sent an expedition across the desert from Nineveh and attacked nim in the rear. It was a difficult enterprise, tracking desert tribes to their oases, but the expedition reached Damascus with great spoil. The army, then reinforced, turned south, sweeping the borders of Bedouin, and attacking Kedarene or Nabatæan settlements. Everywhere the chiefs were killed or taken prisoner, and the spoil was such as to glut the market in Assyria, so that a camel could be bought for half a shekel, or a shekel of silver. Relieved in this way of pressure from the east, the garrisons and vassal states in the west were able to subdue minor risings in Ushu and Akku. Doubtless the fear of the Arabs held in check the desire for freedom in other states. Those of any note were faithful, unless it may be the unfortunate Manasseh, who was taken captive by the Assyrians and carried in chains to Babylon (2 Chron. xxxii. 11).

Ashur-bânipal's northern neighbours gave him some trouble. He had friendly relations with Rusas II. and Sarduris IV. of Urartu, who doubtless still feared their northern invaders. The Mannai, doubtless unable to resist them, were still aggressive towards the south. Their king, Akhsheri, held out bravely against an Assyrian expedition. When defeated he fled, but his subjects rose against him and put him to death. Then Ashur-bânipal set up Ualli as a vassal king. The chiefs of the Medes and Sakhi and the prince of Andaria, in Lubdi, rebelled and were subdued. Gyges had fallen in war with the Gimirri under Tugdamme, and his son, Ardys, appealed for help to Assyria. He and his Assyrian reinforcements defeated and killed Tugdamme (B.C. 645). But in the north, Sennacherib's and Esarhaddon's dispositions for defence held good generally.

Ashur-bânipal's own accounts cease about B.C. 640. They leave us in much doubt as to the exact date of many events, and the usual sources of history fail us for this period. Greek traditions of Sardanapallos, doubtless distant reminiscences of this reign, point to ease and indulgence, but we have no contemporary records.

If one may read between the lines he was a peacefully disposed, cultured, leisurely man, who left war to his warriors. They served him well. He boasts of his warlike expeditions, and naturally takes credit for his army's successes. But he probably made few campaigns himself. He seems to have suffered from ill-health, and the persistent rebellions, in spite of his successes, may be explained by rumours of his insecure tenure of life.

He gloried in the well-being of his faithful people. He pictures the blessings of abundant harvests and peaceful prosperity, in which he gloried almost as much as in the success of his army. He always professes to be greatly hurt by treachery and rebellion, which he knew must be punished, but he really seems to have felt it was unexpected and undeserved.

He was a great builder, and most of the cities in Assyria and Babylonia still furnish traces of his restorations and improvements. His chief claim to our respect is based on his patronage of learning and to his collections now in the British Museum and known as the Kouyunjik collections, from the place where they were found in Nineveh, are our principal source for the literature of Assyria and Babylonia.

The library for which Ashur-bânipal is so justly

famous was compiled from every possible source. We have preserved a letter which was sent to the mayor of Sippara ordering him to take with him certain named officials and such people as he knew well of, and to seek out all the tablets which were in their houses and all the tablets stored in the temple of Êzida, specifying certain series of tablets, astronomical omens, incantations, amulets, all relating to war, spells, prayers, stone inscriptions, and rare tablets, such as were to be found on their route that did not exist in Assyria, and send them to the king. Warrants were sent to the officials in charge of the municipal and palace offices. No one was to withhold tablets. The fact that some of the series of tablets named here are in the library, as now preserved in the British Museum, make it very likely that Ashur-bânipal was the king who sent this order.

There were tens of thousands of clay tablets arranged on shelves for easy consultation, and furnished with lists of titles or catalogues. Apart from the masterpieces of all ages in both Sumerian and Semitic Babylonian, the collections of omens, astronomical portents, the mathematical, grammatical, linguistic tablets of all sorts, forming dictionaries, lists of synonyms, comments or scholia, are still invaluable for the understanding of other texts. The library served also as a registry of contracts, deeds and other documents relating

to the transfer of property. There were stored
hundreds of letters to and from the king, despatches
from the governors of different provinces reporting
public affairs, copies or fragments of ancient inscriptions, lists of eponyms. Long lists of countries,
towns, rivers, mountains, with notes of their position, products and characteristics, formed a sort of
geographical section.

It appears to have been originally situated in the
temple of Nabû, at Kalah, and then transferred to
the temple of the same god at Nineveh. Nabû was
especially patron of the scribe's craft, the god of
wisdom and letters.

The tablets written for the library usually bore
an inscription, often engraved or cut in, after the
tablet was baked, with the words, "Property of
Ashur-bânipal king of hosts, king of Assyria." Many
contain a colophon, giving the tablet's place in its
series, the name of the writer, and often a date, and
more or less of the following formula :—

"Palace of Ashur-bânipal, king of the universe,
king of Assyria, who puts his trust in Ashur and
Bêlit, whom Nabû and Tashmetum have given an
open ear (clear understanding), who has acquired
a bright eye, with the exquisite skill of the tablet
writer, which none of the kings my forefathers (or
predecessors) have learned, the wisdom of Nabû so
far as is written therein with the stroke of the stylus,

ARCHITECTURAL ORNANMTS

BRONZE REPOUSSÉ WORK.

I have written on tablets, that I may read it and learn it, and have laid it up in my palace. I, the ruler who has learned the light of Ashur the king of the gods. (These are for the reading and learning of all who see them.) Who ever shall take them away or deface them or write his name in the place of my name may (such and such gods in various ways) curse him and root out his seed from the earth."

ASHUR-ÊTIL-ILÂNI, B.C. 626.—Ashur-bânipal's two sons, Ashur-êtil-ilâni and Sin-shar-ishkun, succeeded him on the throne, but which of them was his immediate successor is not known. It is usual to assume that Ashur-êtil-ilâni was. Of actual history we have no Assyrian record. We are left to conclude from other sources what its course must have been. The empire gradually slipped from the grasp of its rulers. In Egypt Psammetichus withheld his tribute, and in alliance with Gyges of Lydia procured Carian mercenaries to overthrow his Egyptian rivals and found the twenty-sixth dynasty. The continued incursion of fresh hordes in the north enabled a congeries of peoples to form the Medes who gradually acquired power there and in Elam, now too weak to repel them.

Ashur-êtil-ilâni built a temple of Nabû in Kalah. The remains of his palace are significant of a great decline in wealth. They appear bare and small in comparison with those of his line. He probably continued to use his father's buildings, which were magnificent enough. Two small records of his, grants of large estates to two of his great officials, who earned his gratitude by watching over his youth and suppressing rebellions, speak for the existence of a disturbed reign. One of these, his commander-in-chief, Sin-shum-lishir, appears to be the same who later claimed to be king of Assyria, and was so acknowledged at least for eight months in Nippur. Ashur-êtil-ilâni reigned for at least six years, as attested by dated documents from Nippur. These show that he, at least nominally, held northern Babylonia during the first six years of Nabopolassar's reign.

SIN-SHAR-ISHKUN. — Sin-shar-ishkun, brother of Ashur-êtil-ilâni, reigned for the remainder of the time until the fall of Nineveh. It seems probable that Sin-shum-lishir made a bid for the sovereignty and was acknowledged king in Nippur for eight months. Sin-shar-ishkun, however, evidently overcame this rivalry, for documents are dated in his second and third years at Sippara, which he must have held so long against Nabopolassar, and in his seventh year at Erech. He also has left a grant of lands to a deserving official of his reign, but it throws little light on history. His building inscriptions, of which we possess a few, are drawn up in much the same terms as was usual with the Assyrian kings, but are too fragmentary for us even to identify the buildings.

THE FALL OF NINEVEH.—We may regard our sources of information as a manifold tradition. Nahum, the Hebrew prophet, was a contemporary of the events, but his prophecies scarcely enlighten us much as to the history. Nabonidus makes a few references, and he was only a couple of generations later, but, of course, shared Babylonian prejudices. The statements of Nabopolassar are important, but not very explicit.

Berosus should have had access to authentic contemporary notices, and would be our best authority if we were sure that Abydenus or Ktesias extracted from him with care. Their accounts we only know at second hand. Herodotus gives with fullness of detail a tradition, derived from the Medes and Persians. According to him Deioces—compare the Mannai Daiukku—the founder of the Median kingdom, about the beginning of the seventh century, was succeeded by his son, Phraortes, who subdued the Persians. He then attacked Assyria, but was defeated and lost his life. His son, Cyaxares, re-organised the Median army, and proceeded against Nineveh to avenge his father. He had defeated the Assyrian army, and was besieging Nineveh, when the Scythians, led by Madyes, invaded Media. He raised the siege and attacked the Scythians, who defeated him, and then overran Mesopotamia as far as the borders of Egypt. They were bought off by Psammetichus. Their rule lasted twenty-eight years. Cyaxares recovered his kingdom by slaying the Scythian leaders assembled at a banquet. Then he took Nineveh and so put an end to Assyrian power.

As far as we gather from the fragments of Berosus preserved in Greek writers, Sardanapallus, as they call Ashur-bânipal, was succeeded by Sarakos, obviously Sin-shar-ishkun. Hearing that an army like a swarm of locusts was advancing from the sea, he sent Busalosoros, who may be Nabopolassar, his general, to hold Babylon. The latter, however, allied himself with the Medes, and married his son, Nebuchadnezzar, to the daughter of the Median prince, Ashdakos, and himself attacked Nineveh. Sarakos, hearing of the rebellion and advancing attack, set fire to his palace and perished in the flames. Another tradition states that the Babylonian chief united with the Medes in a rebellion again Sardanapallus and shut him up in Nineveh three years. Then in the third year the Tigris swept away part of the walls of the city, and the king in despair heaped up the treasures of his palace upon a funeral pyre 400 feet high, and offered himself to death in the fire, along with his wives.

Nabopolassar claims to be king of Babylon and to

have conquered the Shubarî. If that term be used
in its early sense it must have included Assyria. If
in a later meaning, as applied to a people north-east
of Assyria, Nineveh must have fallen or at least been
powerless. Nabonidus does tell us a little more.
He says that Nabopolassar found a helper in the
king of the Umman-manda, a term used to describe
northern invaders, with no special ethnic meaning.
They ruined the temples of the gods of Assyria, and
the cities on the border of Akkad which were hostile
to the king of Akkad and had not come to his help,
and laid waste their sanctuaries. We may conclude
that the Babylonians were at war with Assyria, and
in alliance with the Umman-manda, yet not the
Babylonians, but this other people, really destroyed
Assyria. These Umman-manda may well be the
Scythian hordes of Herodotus.

It is difficult to harmonise all these accounts, and
even the exact date of the fall of Nineveh is not
certain. It is usually set at B.C. 606.

It may well be that not even the finest Assyrian
generals in the best period of Assyrian power could
have averted such a catastrophe. For no one was
found able to stand the onslaught of the Scythians.
It is, however, natural to suppose that the civil war
in Shamash-shum-ukin's time, the wars with Egypt
and Elam, had so weakened Assyria and scattered its
resources that it was in a powerless condition. All

must remain a matter of speculation until further light is thrown on the actual events. The people from the sea suggest an invasion of Lower Babylonia by the Chaldæans of the Sea land who, in Merodach-Baladan's time, had taxed even Sargon to his utmost.

SENNACHERIB SUPERINTENDIN

THE TRANSFER OF A COLOSSUS.

BIBLIOGRAPHY

GOODSPEED, PROFESSOR G. S. *A History of the Babylonians and Assyrians.* London : Smith, Elder & Co. 1903. For earlier works, see the Bibliography on pp. 385-404.

KING, L. W. *Records of the Reign of Tukulti-Ninib I., king of Assyria, about B.C. 1275.* London : Luzac & Co. 1904.

KING, L. W. *Chronicles concerning early Babylonian Kings.* 2 vols. London : Luzac & Co. 1907.

TOFFTEEN, O. A. *Ancient Chronology.* Chicago : University of Chicago Press. 1907.

SCHNABEL, P. *Studien zur babylonisch-assyrische Chronologie. Mitteilungen der Vorderasiatischen Gesellschaft.* Leipzig : J. C. Hinrichs. 1908. Full Bibliography.

UNGNAD, A. *Untersuchungen zu den Urkunden aus Dilbat. Beiträge zur Assyriologie.* Leipzig : J. C. Hinrichs. 1909.

SCHEIL, V. *Annales de Tukulti-Ninip II.* Paris : Champion. 1909.

KING, L. W. *Cuneiform Texts from Babylonian Tablets, etc., in the British Museum,* Vol. 26. New Prism of Sennacherib. London : Trustees of British Museum. 1909.

DELITZSCH, FR. *Keilschrift texte aus Assur historischen Inhalts.* Leipzig : J. C. Hinrichs. 1911.

Numerous articles in the *Orientalistische Litteratur-Zeitung,* Berlin, Wolf Peiser Verlag, deal with new material.

157

INDEX

Abdadana, 102

Abdi-milkutti, king of Sidon, 137

Abech (= Ebekh ?) Mount, 13

Abeshu', 8th king of First Dynasty of Babylon, 113

Abi-ba'al, king of Samsimuruna, 138

Abu-Habba, mod. name of Sippara, q.v.

Abu-shahrein, mod. name of Eridu, q.v.

Abydenus, author, 123, 153

Adad, weather or sky god, 36

—— god of Ekallâte, 25, 78, 129

—— temple in Asshur, 141

—— treasure house, 76

Adad-apli-iddina, king of Babylon, 79

Adad-bêl-ukin, viceroy, 59

Adad-idri, Hadad-ezer, king of Damascus, 95

Adad-nâdin-akhi, see Adad-shum-utsur

Adad-nirari I., king of Assyria, 23, 48, 49, 53, 57, 58, 59, 60, 61, 62, 63, 80, 137, 153

—— II., king of Assyria, 79

—— III., ,, ,, ,, 80, 81

—— IV., ,, ,, ,, 37, 39, 41, 42, 48, 102, 120

—— V., king of Assyria, 104, 105

Adad-shum-lishir, 66, 67

Adad-shum-utsur, king of Babylon, 66, 67, 68

Adasi, early ruler, 11, 35, 36, 37, 38

Adaush, 73

Adhem, river, 12

Adrammelech, son Sennacherib, 130

Agade, city, 136

Agusi, land, 105, 107

Ahab, king of Israel, 17, 95

Ahaz, king of Judah, 4, 109, 110

Aiaru, 2nd month, 106

Aitakama, king of Mitanni, 54

Akarsallu, city, 69, 77

Akhiababa, upstart ruler of Carchemish, 85

Akhlami, Aramæan tribe, 51, 62, 63, 69, 74

Akhsheri, king of Mannai, 147

Akhûni, king of Bît Adini, 94

Akhimilki, king of Ashdod, 138

Akhimiti, ,, ,, , 114

Akkad, Northern Babylonia, 65, 66, 77, 81, 101, 142, 155

Akku, in Palestine (= Accho), 146

Aksu, river, 12

Allabra, land, 92, 102

Alshe, district, 53

Alzi, district, 71

Amadâni, 92

Amanus, range, 80, 91, 95

Amalek, Meluhha, q.v., 114

Amedi, city, 59, 92, 99, 103
Amekà, 87
Amenophis II., king of Egypt, 54, 55, 56
—— III., king of Egypt, 54, 56
—— IV., king of Egypt, 53, 54, 56, 60
Ammati, 87
Ammaush, 73
Amminadbi, king of Ammon, 140
Ammon, land, 95, 109, 125, 138, 140
Amorite, people, 10, 39
Amurru = west land, 102
Ana-Ashur-taklaku, ancestor of Sennacherib, 3
Andaria, land, 147
Andia, land, 102
Annals, 107
Anu, god, 46, 103
Anu and Adad, temple in Asshur, 13, 24, 45, 71, 76
Apki, city, 78
Apri, R., 91
Aqaba, gulf, 110
Arabia, land, Arab, Arabians, 33, 95, 108, 109, 114, 125, 126, 138, 143, 146, 147
Arabic language, 16
Arakhtu, canal, 129
Aramæans, people, 57, 63, 74, 80, 93, 101, 107, 113, 118, 124, 142, 143
Aramaic language, 51
Arame, king of Urartu, 97
Arapkha, city, 105
Arashtua, 87
Araziash, city, 100, 102
Araziqu, 75
Arbaki, 87

Arbela, city, 13, 28, 31, 32, 84, 97, 99, 131
Archons, 26, 31
Ardys, king of Lydia, 147
Ardi-Bêlit, crown prince, 130
Ardupa, 86
Argistis I., king of Urartu, 104
—— II.,   ,,   ,,   ,, 116, 117
Aribi, land, 114
Aridi, city, 99
Arik-dên-Bêl = Arik-dên-ilu, king of Assyria, 23, 61, 80
Arime, 77
Arini, city, 74
Armenia (= Urartu, q.v.), 5, 14, 96, 114, 116, 134, 136
Arnûni, city, 61
Arpad, city, 103, 105, 108, 113
Arqania, land, 92
Artashshumara, king of Mitanni, 54
Artatama I., king of Mitanni, 54, 55
—— II., king of Mitanni, 54
Aruma, Mount, 72
Arvad, city, 77, 91, 95, 137, 140, 142
Aryan affinities of Mitanni, 52
Arzashku, city, 97
Arzukhina, city, 77
Asalli, 91
Asaniu, Mount, 73
Ashdakos, king of Medes, 154
Ashdod, city, 114, 126, 138
Ashdudimma, city, 114
Ashguza, Ashkenaz, 137
Ashir, Ashur, q.v., 6, 13, 49
Ashsha, city, 92
Ashur, national god of Assyria, 2, 6, 24, 28, 33, 34, 36, 40, 44, 150, 151

Ashur, temple of, in Asshur, 23, 35, 38, 41, 45, 47
—— —— in Nineveh, 134
Ashur-bânipal, king of Assyria, 132, 133, 154
—— reign, 140, 151
—— his library in Nineveh, 48
Ashur-bêl-kala, king of Assyria, 78, 80
Ashur-bêl-nishêshu I., king of Assyria, 48, 49
—— II., king of Assyria, 49, 57
Ashur-gamilia, ancestor of Sennacherib, 3
Ashur-dân I., king of Assyria, 24, 45, 69, 78
—— II., 80
—— III., 104
Ashur - dânin - apli, king of Assyria, 99
Ashur-etil-ilâni, king of Assyria, 151, 152
Ashur-ilu-muballitsu, son of Sennacherib, 132
Ashur-irbi, king of Assyria, 47
Ashur-munik, son of Sennacherib, 130
Ashur-nâdin-akhê I., king of Assyria, 53, 54, 55, 59, 78
—— II., king of Assyria, 57, 59, 62
Ashur-nâdin-shûm, king of Babylon, 127, 128, 130
Ashur-natsir-pal I., king of Assyria, 66, 96
—— II., king of Assyria, 79
—— III., ,, ,, ,, 83, 92
Ashur-nirari I., king of Assyria, 39, 40, 45, 49
—— II., king of Assyria, 47
—— III., ,, ,, ,, 66, 68

Ashur - nirari IV., king of Assyria, 105
Ashur-rabi I., king of Assyria, 47, 49
—— II., king of Assyria, 79, 81
Ashur - rêsh - ishi I., king of Assyria, 24, 69, 70, 78
—— II., king of Assyria, 58, 79
Ashur - rîm - nishêshu, king of Assyria, 35, 39, 47, 49
Ashur-shar-etir, son of Sennacherib, 130
Ashur-uballit, king of Assyria, 53, 55, 56, 57, 59, 60
Asia Minor, 2, 96, 123, 136
Asini, king, 61
Asiru, people, 12
Askelon, city, 110, 125, 137
Asmu, city, 90
Asshur, land, 6, 7, 13, 36, 37, 47, 48, 55
—— city, 2, 6, *passim*
—— new city, 48
—— city wall, 35, 39, 41, 43, 45, 47
—— cemetery, 58
—— temple of Ashur, 41, 46, 62, 64
—— —— Bêl shiplra, 45
—— —— Bêl, 46
—— —— Bît shukhuri, 45
—— —— Ishtar, 40, 41, 42, 45
—— well in, 59
—— *Zikkurat*, 41
—— viceroys, 58
—— son of Shem, 1
Asshurai = Assyrians, 5
Assyria, Hebrew traditions, 1, 2, 3, 4, 5
—— native traditions, 3, 7

L

Assyria, name, 5
—— land, 8, 11
—— culture, 97, 137
Assyrians, people, provinces, etc., 1, 3, 4, 5, 6, 8, *passim*
—— language, 7, 16, 38, 97
—— monuments, 17, 18, 21
—— architecture, 123
—— colonists, 124
Atalur, Mount, 47
Athens, city, 26
Athenian temple, 123
Atlila, Mount, 88
Atmesu, king of Tamesu, 138
Atuma, Mount, 73
Aushpia, *see* Ushpia, 12, 23, 35, 38, 41
Aza, king of Mannai, 115
Azi-ba'al, king of Arvad, 142
Aziru, Mount, 87
Azu, Mount, 73
Azuri, king of Ashdod, 114

Ba'al, king of Tyre, 36, 137, 138, 139, 140, 141
Babite, pass, 86, 87
Babylon, city, 1, 12, *passim*
—— captured, 3
—— destroyed, 129
—— war with, 41, 101, 107, 118
Babylonia, 1, 2, 3, *passim*
Babylonian Chronicle, 52, 66, 111
—— language, 7, 16, 50, 149
—— people, 8, 33, 36, 41, 42, 43
—— culture, 10, 32
Bagdatti, king of Umildish, 115
Ba'li, city, 103
Bàra, city, 87
Bar-Requb, king of Sama'al, 109
Bartatûa, king of Medes, 136
Barzanishtun, city, 92

Bàsha-Ashir I., king of Assyria, 39
—— II., king of Assyria, 40, 45
Bau-akh-iddina, king of Babylon, 101
Bavian, city, 25
Bazu, district, 138
Bedouin, people, 146
Beer, early decipherer, 16
Behistun, rock, 16
Bêl a god = Marduk, *q.v.*, 38
—— altar, 46, 83
—— hand of Bêl, 111, 113, 118
Bêl-bani, king of Assyria, 35, 36, 37
Bêl-dabi, king of Assyria, 42
Bêl-ibni, king of Babylon, 125, 127
Bêlit, goddess, 150
Bêl-kabi, king of Assyria, 23, 38, 39, 42, 43
Bêl-kapkapu I., king of Assyria 37, 38, 42, 102
—— II., king of Assyria, 42
Bêl-kudur-utsur, king of Assyria, 68
Bêl-nirari, king of Assyria, 60, 61
Bêl shipria, god, temple in Asshur, 45
Bêl-tartsi-anma, viceroy, 103
Bêl-uballit, Tartan, 59
Bêlus, eponymous hero, 2
Benê, 51
Berlin Musem, 50
Berosus, author, 2, 153, 154
Beshri, Mount, 74
Beth, in place names, 51
Biblical notices, 5, 17, 130, *cf.* Hebrew tradition
Bikni, range, 107
Bisuru, Mount, 90

Bit Adini (= Beth Eden), 12, 51, 84, 85, 90, 91, 94, 97
Bit Agusi, 95, 105, 107
Bit Amukkani, 12, 107, 110
Bit Asiri, land, 12
Bit Bakhiari, 90
Bit Daiukku, state, 115
Bit Dakkuri, 118, 135
Bit Iakin, 12, 111, 118, 119, 127
Bit Khalupi, 82, 84, 89
Bit pagri, 58
Bit Ridûti, city, 101
Bit Shabaia, 89
Bit Shilâni, 107
Bit Shukhuri, temple in Asshur, 45
Bit Zamâni, 86, 89
Black obelisk, 93, 99
Boghaz koï, place, 49, 52, 53
Borsippa, city, 101, 102, 118, 134
Botta, explorer, 18
Boundary treaties, 48, 56
British Museum, 17, 47, 48, 66, 67, 148, 149
Buba, king, 84
Budu-il, king of Ammon, 138
Buliani pass, 86
Bunisa, 87
Burnaburiash, Kassite, king of Babylon, 48, 56, 57
Burnouf, decipherer, 16
Busalosoros, general, 154
Butsusu, king of Nure, 138
Byblos, city, 91, 137

Cairo, city, 50
Calah, city, see Kalah
Calno, city, 108
Canon, Eponym, cf. Eponym lists, 26, 104
—— Ptolemy's, 27
Cappadocia, land, 5, 12, 13, 71

Carchemish, city, 31, 63, 74, 90, 91, 94, 95, 99, 108, 116
Carians people, 142, 151
Caspian, Sea, 115
Chabur = Habor = Habur, river, 61
Chaldæa, Chaldæans, 12, 90, 94, 101, passim
Choser, river, 14, 130, 132
Chronicles, Babylonian, 52
Cilicia, country, 5, 11, 110, 116, 123, 137, 142
Cilician gates, 123
Commagene, country, 31, 65, 71, 72, 84, 88, 92, 107, 108, 116, 117
Consuls, Roman, 31
Cush = Ethiopia, 139
Cyaxares, king of Medes, 153, 154
Cydnus, river, 123
Cyprus, island, 117, 125, 128, 137, 138

Dagara, 86
Daieni, land, 74
Daiukku, king of Mannai, 153
Damascus, city, 4, 94, 95, 96, 102, 104, 108, 109, 110, 113, 146
Damasu, king of Curium, 138
Damdamusa, city, 85, 86, 92
Damusi, king of Qarti-khadashti, 138
Daria, 73
Darius Hystaspes, 16
Datebir, city, 100
Deioces, king, 153
Diarbekr, city, 63
Di'ibina, city, 100
Dilmun, island, 119
Diodorus, author, 131
Dira, 89
Dirria, 92
Dummeti, city, 90

Duppani, Mount, 91
Dûra, 87
Dûr-Ashur, city, 88
Dûr-ilu, city, 101, 103, 113, 134, 143
Dûr-Katlime, city, 89
Dûr-Kurigalzu, city, 77, 82, 107
Dûr-Papsukkal, city, 101
Dûr-Sargon, city, 14, 18
Dûr Sharrukin, 119

Ê-am-kurkurra, temple of Bêl in Asshur, 46
Easharru, Mitanni god, 11
Ebikh, Mount, 100
Edial, city, 138
Edir, river, 87
Edom, country, 95, 102, 109, 114, 125, 137
Egi, Mount, 84
Egiba, eponymous hero, 3
Egypt, land, 5, 11, 50, 51, 52, 53, 54, 55, 56, 96, 111, 113, 114, 124, 125, 138, 139, 140, 141, 142, 143, 151, 154, 155
Egyptian chronology, 27, 51 ; inscriptions, 49
Ekallâte, city, 25, 58, 59, 78, 129
Ekishtura, king of Edial, 138
Ekron, city, 125, 126, 137
Elam, Elamites, 5, 9, 11, 12, 13, 27, 35, 38, 100, 101, 107, 113, 115, 118, 119, 123, 124, 127, 128, 129, 135, 136, 141, 142, 143, 144, 145, 151, 155
Elaniu, 87
Ellipi, land, 102, 115, 123
Eltekeh city, 125
Elukhat, city, 62, 62
Elul, 6th month, 111
Engidu, mythical hero, 3
Enzi, city, 99

Eponyms, Eponymy, 13, 30, 31
—— Canon, 26, 80, 105, 107
—— lists, 30, 99, 103, 104, 111
Erba-Adad I., king of Assyria, 49, 57
—— Mausoleum, 58, 78
—— II., king of Assyria, 57, 59, 68
Erech, city, 9, 36, 118, 119, 134, 143, 144, 145, 152
Eresu, king of Sillu, 138
Eridu, city, 6
Erini, land, 104
Erishum, king of Assyria, 23, 39, 40, 41, 42, 43, 44
Esagila, temple of Marduk in Babylon, 65, 129
Esarhaddon, king of Assyria, 4, 23, 24, 35, 36, 37, 38, 39, 41, 42, 43, 44, 106, 126, 129, 132, 133-139, 140, 143, 146, 147
Ethiopia, land, 36, 114, 125, 139, 141
Etini, Mount, 87
Euphrates, river, 9, 60, 63, 74, 75, 81, 82, 84, 89, 90, 91, 92, 102, 107, 108, 118, 123, 128
Europe, 7, 18
Eusebius, author, 3
Ezida, temple of Nabû at Borsippa, 149

First Dynasty of Babylon, 12, 35, 39, 40, 43, 52, 133
Flood, the, 3

Galilee, land, 112
Gambuli, people, 118, 143
Gamgum, land, 108, 117
Gananati, river, 100, 101, 104
Gath, city, 114
Gaza, city, 109, 113, 126, 137

German explorations, 18
Gilgamesh, mythical hero, 3
Gilu-khipa, Hittite princess, 54
Gilzani, land, 84, 87, 97
Gimirri = Gomer = Cimmerians, people, 116, 136, 137, 142, 147
Gizilbunda, land, 100, 102
Gozan = Guzana, 112
Great Sea, 46, 102
Greeks, 2, 123, 147; traditions, 154
Grotefend, decipherer, 15
Gudea, king of Lagash, 32
Gurgurri, gate at Asshur, 78, 98
Guzana = Gozan, 102, 103, 105; land
Gyges, king of Lydia, 142, 147, 151

Habor, river, 4
Habur, cf. Chabor, 75, 82, 85, 89, 90; river
Hadrach, city, 104, 105
Hague, The, 103
Halah, city, 4, 61, 112
Hamath, city, 94, 95, 96, 108, 112, 113
Hammurabi, sixth king of 1st Dynasty of Babylon, 10, 37, 41, 42, 43, 45, 52, 130
Hanno, king of Gaza, 109, 113
Haran, city, 46, 57, 59, 61, 62, 63, 75, 105, 106, 139
Hauran, district, 97
Hazael, king of Arabia, 138
—— king of Damascus, 95, 96
Hazu, district in Arabia, 138
Hebrew tradition, 1, 127, 153
—— language, 16
—— people, 1, 2

Hermon, Mount, 96
Herodotus, author, 2, 103, 127, 133, 153
Hezekiah, king of Judah, 125, 126
Hincks, decipherer, 16
Hirom, king of Tyre, 108
Hit, city, 82
Hittites, people, 27, 49, 51, 52, 53, 54, 63, 71, 72, 75, 84, 86, 91, 102, 123, 133
Hosea, king of Israel, 4, 49, 109, 111

Iakhani, 91
Iakinlu, king of Arvad, 140, 141, 142
Ialman, Mount, 81, 100
Ialuna, district, 59, 103
Iaraqi, Mount, 91
Iasubakula, people, 61
Iasubigalli, people, 61
Iaturi, Mount, 91
Iaudi, land, 108
Iauri, people, 62
Igur-kapkapu, king of Assyria, 38, 39, 46
Ikausu, king of Ekron, 137
Ikunum, king of Assyria, 40, 41, 44
Ilat, 89
Illubru, state, 123
Ilu-bi'di, king of Hamath, 112, 113
Ilu-ibni, 85
Ilu-ittia, viceroy, 58
Ilushumma, king of Assyria, 23, 26, 35, 37, 39, 40, 41
Imgur-Bêl, city, 14
Indabigash, king of Elam, 144, 145
Indo-European race, 98
Indra, Mitanni god, 52

Ingirâ, city, 123
Ionians, people, 123
Iranzu, king of Mannai, 115
Irkhuleni, king of Hamath, 95
Irishum, king of Assyria, 23, 41 = Erishum
Irnina, goddess, 70
Irria, 69, 88
Irridu, city, 63
Isalla, 85
Ishme-Dagan, king of Isin, 10
—— I., king of Assyria, 24, 44, 45
—— II., ,, ,, 45
Ishpaka, king of Ashguza, 137
Ishpuinis, king of Urartu, 97
Ishtar, goddess, 11, 40, 70
—— her temple at Asshur, 40, 41, 42, 76
—— of Nineveh, 44, 53, 64, 79
Ishtarâte, pass, 88
Isin, city, 9, 10
Israel, land, 4, 94, 95, 96, 102, 108, 109, 111, 112
Isua, 73
Itamara, king of Saba, 114
Itoba'al, king of Sidon, 125, 137
Itu = Hit, city, 58
Itu'a, people, 103, 104, 107, 112
Ituandar, king of Paphos, 138
Izduia, city, 100

Jailu, king of Arabia, 138, 146
Jazarmash, Cilician god, 11
Jebel, Hamrin, Mount, 13
Jebel, Maglub, Mount, 119, 130
Jehu, king of Israel, 17, 95
Jerusalem, city, 4, 110, 126, 138
Judah, land, 4, 95, 109, 110, 114, 125, 126, 137, 140

Kadashman - Bêl, king of Babylon, 56

Kadashman - kharbe, king of Babylon, 60
Kakzi, city, 87
Kalah, city, 1, 2, 11, 14, 17, 31, 37, 58, 64, 83, 87, 89, 90, 99, 102, 103, 106, 119, 132, 133, 134, 150, 151
Kali-Teshup, king, 72
Kammanu, land, 117
Kandalanu, king of Babylon, 144
Kaprabi, city, 90
Karaburiash, 77
Kara-indash, king of Babylon, 48, 57
Kara-khardash, king of Babylon, 56, 60
Karania, 92
Kar-Ashur, city, 107
Kar-Ashur-natsirpal, city, 100
Karduniash, Kassite Babylonia, 48, 57, 66, 69, 88, 90, 100
Kar-Esarhaddon, city, 137
Karkashi, land, 136
Karnê, city, 100
Kar-Shalmaneser, city, 99
Karsibutai, district, 100
Kar-Tukulti-Ninip, 58, 59, 65, 66
Kashi, people, 72
Kashiari, range, 63, 71, 85, 88, 92, 97
Kashtarit, king of Gimirri, 136
Kashtiliash II., king of Babylon, 25, 65
Kassite, people, 12, 25, 55, 60, 61, 62, 89, 122
—— dynasty, 48, 51, 52
Kati, king of Tabal, 99
Kedarenes, people, 146
Khaldia, land, 96
Khaldis, a god, 96
Khallushu, king of Elam, 128
Khalman, city, 94, 95

Khalule, city, 129, 133
Khalzi-lukha, city, 85
Khamurza, Mount, 91
Khani = Mitanni, 52
Khanigalbat = Mitanni, 52, 54, 63, 74, 134
Khania, 73
Kharida, 90
Kharkhar, city, 100, 102
Kharmesh, river, 89
Kharri, people, 52
Khartishri, 87
Khashmar, pass, 87
Khatti = Hittites, 53, 138
Khatusar, king of the Hittites, 72
Khazazi, city, 91, 103
Khidalu, land, 143
Khilakku = Cilicia, q.v.
Khindanu, city, 82, 85, 89, 90, 99
Khiranu, 92
Khorsabad gate, at Nineveh, 131
Khubushki, land, 84, 87, 97, 100, 103
Khuduni, land, 86
Khulun, 84
Khumbanigash, king of Elam, 143, 144
Khumma-khaldash I., king of Elam, 135
—— II., king of Elam, 135
—— III., king of Elam, 145
Khumri = Omri = Israel, land, 102
Khunusa, 74
Khurshitu, land, 12
Khuzirina, 59, 92
Kibaki, 88
Kigallu, 79
Kikia, king of Assyria, 11, 12, 35, 38, 39
Kiki-Bêl, king of Assyria, 44
Kili-Teshup, 72

Kinabu, 85
Kinaki, city, 100
Kinalia, city, 108
Kipina, 90
Kir, land, 109
Kirbit, city in Elam, 141
Kiribti-abâni, city, 101
Kirkhi, land, 73, 84, 86, 88, 92
Kirruri, land, 84
Kirûa, king of Illubru, 123
Kisb, city, 103, 124
Kishtau, land, 107
Kisirtu, 87
Kisu, king of Sillua, 138
Kitrusi, city, 138
Kouyunjik, 66, 67, 130, 132, 148
Ktesias, author, 153
Kubbu, 92
Kudru, 87
Kudina, city, 61
Kudur-nanhundi, king of Elam, 128, 129
Kukunu, 89
Kullani = Calno, city, 108
Kummukh, see Commagene
Kunulua, city, 91
Kurdistan, mts., 14
Kuri, city, 138
Kurigalzu, king of Babylon, 56, 60, 61
Kustaspi, king of Commagene, 108
Kutha, city, 94, 101, 102, 107, 112, 144
Kuti, people, 69, 107
Kutila, city, 61

Laban, district, 46
Lachish, city, 126
Lagash, city, 32
Lakhiru, city, 101
Lallu river, 87

Laqê, city, 82, 84, 85, 90
Lara, 87
Larsa, city, 12
Lassen, decipherer, 16
Latin, 7
Layard, explorer, 16, 17, 134
Lebanon, Mts., 46, 89, 91
Liburna, 84
Litau, people, 107
London Museum, 50
Longperier, decipherer, 16
Lubdi, people, 62, 77, 147
Lukutu, city, 91
Luli, king of Tyre, 125
Lulume, people, 62, 63, 69, 103
Lutipris, king of Urartu, 96
Lybia, land, 143
Lydia, land, 142
Lygdamis, king of Gimirri, 136

Madai=Medes, people, 98, 102, 103
Madara, 88
Madaranzu, 88
Madyes, king of Scythians, 153
Maganuba, city, 105, 120
Magarisi, city, 89
Maisa, 91
Makhalata, 91
Malatia, city, 52, 63, 96, 108
Maliki, city, 101
Mallanu, 92
Manasseh, king of Judah, 137, 140, 147
Mannai, people, 98, 100, 103, 115, 136, 137, 147, 153
Mantsuate, city, 103
Marad, city, 104
Marduk, god, 36, 55, 65, 66, 67 = Merodach, 135
Marduk-apli-iddina = Merodach Baladan, q.v.

Marduk-balatsu-ikbi, king of Babylon, 101
Marduk-bêl-usâte, king of Babylon, 93, 94
Marduk-ishmeani, viceroy, 58
Marduk-nâdin-akhê, king of Babylon, 25, 77, 78, 129
Marduk-nâdin-shum, king of Babylon, 93, 94
Marduk-shapik-zêr-mâti, king of Babylon, 78
Marduk-shum-iddin, king of Babylon, 102
Marduk-ushezib, king of Babylon, 127
Marduk-zakir-shum, king of Babylon, 124
Marê, 51
Mari', king of Damascus, 102
Mariru, 86
Marriti, 77
Martu, god of Amorites, 76
Matan-Ba'al, king of Arvad, 137, 140
Matiati, 88
Mati-ilu, king of Agusi, 105, 107
Matni, Mount, 89
Mattiuza, king of Mitanni, 53, 54
Mazamûa, land, 98
Media, Medes, 5, 98, 100, 103, 104, 107, 112, 115, 131, 136, 146, 147, 151, 153, 154
Mediterranean Sea, 41, 46, 80, 89, 91, 102, 114, 125
Meluhha, land, 114
Memphis, city, 138, 140
Menahem, king of Israel, 4, 108
Merodach Baladan, king of Bît Iakin, 111, 127
——— king of Babylon, 113, 117, 118, 119, 124, 125, 135, 143, 156

Meshech = Musku, q.v.

Mesopotamia, land, 9, 21, 51, 64, 65, 95, 154

Mesu, land, 88, 100, 102

Mê-Turnat, city, 100, 101

Mildish, city, 72

Milid, city, 97, 116, 117, 136

Milidia, city, 74

Milki-ashapa, king of Byblos, 137

Mita (= Midas?), king of Mus-khi, 115, 116, 117

Mitanni, land, 11, 27, 35, 38, 50, 51, 52, 53, 54, 55, 57, 63, 75, 86

Mithra, god of Mitanni, 52

Mitinti, king of Ashdod, 126

—— king of Askelon, 137

Moab, land, 95, 109, 114, 125, 137

Mosul, city, 25

Muballitat - Sherûa, Assyrian princess, 56

Mukallu, king of Tabal, 141

Munna, city, 102

Munzigana, Mount, 91

Murattash, 93

Mushezib-Marduk, king of Baby-lon, 128, 129

Mushku = Meshech, land, 71, 84, 115, 116, 117

Muski, 82

Musuri, king of Moab, 137

Mutakkil-Nusku, king of As-syria, 24, 69

Mutkinu, 80

Mutsri, in N. Arabia, 109, 111, 113, 114, 125

—— in N. Syria, 74, 95

—— in Egypt, 77

Nabatæans, people, 146

Nabonassar, king of Babylon, 105, 106, 110

Nabonidus, king of Babylon, 153, 155

Nabopolassar, king of Babylon, 152, 153, 154, 155

Nabû, god of letters, 36, 102, 103, 150, 151

Nabû-apli-iddina, king of Baby-lon, 89, 93

Nabû-hêl-shumâte, 144, 145

Nabû-dân, king of Assyria, 66

Nabû-shum-iskun, king of Baby-lon, 81

Nabû-shum-ukin, king of Baby-lon, 110

Nabû-zêr-napishti-lishir, son of Merodach Baladan, 135

Nahr-el-Kelb, river, 139

Nahum, Hebrew prophet, 4, 153

Na'id-Ashur, ancestor of Sen-nacherib, 3

Nairi, land, 11, 58, 65, 73, 86, 88, 89, 99, 100, 101, 102, 108

Namri, land, 103, 104, 105, 106

Namu-bilkhi, city, 61

Nanâ, goddess, 36, 145

Naqara-bani, city, 89

Naqia, queen of Sennacherib, 135, 140

Naram-Sin, king of Akkad, 9

Nazi-bugash, king of Babylon, 60

Nazi-marattash, king of Baby-lon, 62

Nebi Yunus, mound, 132

Nebuchadnezzar I., king of Babylon, 70

—— II., king of Babylon, 154

Necho, king of Egypt, 141

Nergal-ushezib, king of Babylon, 128

Nibarti-Ashur, city, 90

Nigimti, district, 61, 62

Nineveh, city, 1, 2, 4, 10, 11, 14, 17, 25, 26, 28, 29, 31, 32, 41, 44, 53, 58, 59, 63, 64, 79, 83, 84, 85, 99, 119, 120, 122, 123, 126, 127, 128, 129, 130, 132, 133, 134, 137, 141, 146, 148, 150, 152, 153

—— library, 48, 133, 149-151, 153, 154, 155

Ninib, god of war, 83

Ninib - apil - esharra, king of Assyria, 68

Ninib-tukulti-Ashur, king of Assyria, 66, 67, 68

Ninkigal, goddess, 41, 44

Ninus, eponymous hero, 2

Nippur, city, 9, 107, 118, 128, 152

Nipur, Mount, 84, 123

Nirbu, 86

Nirdun, 86, 88

Nisan, first month, 113

Nishpatti-utli, viceroy, 58

Nishtun, city, 84

Nisibis, city, 82

Nispi, Mount, 87

Nitsir, Mount, 87

Nomads, 57

Numme, district, 84

Nure, city, 138

Old Testament, 4, 15

Omri, king of Israel, 17, 95

Opis, city, 77, 128

Orontes, river, 91, 95

Paddira, district, 99

Padi, king of Ekron, 125, 126

Pae, king of Elam, 145

Palestine, land, 4, 50, 102, 109, 112, 113, 114, 119, 124, 125, 126, 146

Panammu, king of Sama'al, 108, 109

Panarus, Mount, 72

Paphos, city, 138

Paqruru, king, 141

Parsûa, Persia, 98, 100, 102

Patesi, a title, 28, 32, 33, 34, 36, 40, 41, 42, 44, 45, 47

Pati-khegalli, canal, 84

Patini, land, 84, 91, 94, 96, 108

Pazita, city, 107

Pekah, king of Israel, 109

Pekod, people, 107

Persia, land, 5

—— Old Persian inscriptions, 15, 16

Persians, people, 98, 115, 136, 153

Persian Gulf, 119

Philistines, people, 109

Phœnicia, land, 109, 111, 123, 125, 128, 137

Phœnicians, 123, 128

Phraortes, king of Medes, 153

Phrygia, land, 136

Pilagura, king of Kitrusi, 138

Pilasqi, people, 62

Piru, king of Mutsri, 113, 114

Pisiris, king of Carchemish, 108, 116

Pitru (Pethor ?), 80

Pitura (Pethor ?), 89

Psammetichus, king of Egypt, 141, 151, 154

Pteria, land, 52

Pudi-ilu, *see* Arik-dân-ilu

Pukhia, king of Khurshitu, 12

Pukudu (Pekod), people, 107

Pûlu, king of Babylon, 106

Purukuzzi, land, 71

Puzur-Ashur I., king of Assyria, 48, 49, 57
—— II., king of Assyria, 49, 57

Qarqar, city, 95, 113
Qarti-khadashti, city, 138
Qatnu, 85, 89
Qaushgabri, king of Edom, 137
Qipani, 91
Quay of Asshur, 80
Quê, land, 95, 96, 108, 116, 117, 123
Qumâni, 74, 75
Qurtê, 72, 73
Quti, people, 62

Radanu, river, 87
Raphia, city, 113
Rapiqu, city, 62, 77
Rask, decipherer, 16
Rawlinson, decipherer, 16
Rehoboth, city, 1, 2, 120
Resen, city, 1, 2
Rezin, king of Damascus, 108, 109, 110
Rhodanus, river, 12
Rîm-Anum, king of Larsa, 12
Rome, city, 31
Ru'a, people, 107
Rubu', people, 107
Ruqukhu, city, 58, 59
Rusas I., king of Urartu, 114, 115, 119
—— II., king of Urartu, 147

Saba, land, 114
Sabæans, people, 109
Sabarain, city, 111
St Martin, decipherer, 16
Sakhi, people, 147
Salla, 92
Sama'al, city, 94, 108, 109, 139

Samaria, city, 4, 31, 111, 112, 113
Sammuramat, queen of Assyria, 42, 58, 102, 103
Samsi, queen of Arabia, 109, 114
Samsi-Adad, king of Assyria, 38, 39, 46
Samsi-muruna, city, 137
Samsuditana, king of Babylon, 39, 52
Samsu-iluna, king of Babylon, 39
Sandasarme, king of Cilicia, 141
Sanduarri, king of Cilicia, 137
Sangara, king of Hittites, 91
Sangura, river, 91
Sapia, city, 110, 111
Saradaush, 73
Sarakos = Sin-shar-ishkun, q.v., 154
Saratini, Mount, 91
Saraush, 73
Sardanapallos = Ashur-bânipal, 147, 154
Sarduris I., king of Urartu, 96
—— II., king of Urartu, 97
—— III., king of Urartu, 107, 108, 114
—— IV., king of Urartu, 147
Sargon, king of Akkad, 9, 41, 119
Sargon I., king of Assyria, see Sharrukin
—— II., king of Assyria, 3, 11, 17, 30, 36, 41, 93, 105, 111, 112-119, 124, 133, 156
Sargonburgh, see Dûr-Sargon
Sargonids, dynasty, 139
Sarrabanu, city, 107
Sashiashai, district, 100
Sattuara, king of Mitanni, 63

172 ANCIENT ASSYRIA

Saulcy, decipherer, 16

Saushatar, king of Mitanni, 53, 54, 55

Scythians, people, 153, 154, 155

Sealand, district, 65, 103, 156

Second Dynasty of Ur, 13

Semiramis, queen of Assyria, 42, 102

Semitic, 7, 8, 9, 10, 11, 12, 16, 33, 35, 37, 39, 51, 149

Sendjirli=Zanjirli on map, 35

Sennacherib, king of Assyria, 3, 4, 17, 24, 25, 36, 58, 61, 68, 116, 122-134, 137, 138, 147

Sepulchres of the kings, 58

Seve, king of Mutsri, 111

Shabako, king of Ethiopia, 114

Shadikani, city, 82, 85, 89

Shadi-Teshup, king, 72

Shagarakti-Shuriash, king of Babylon, 25, 65, 67, 129

Shaknu, title, 34

Shala, goddess, 25, 129

Shalim-akhum, king of Assyria, 40, 41

Shalmaneser I., king of Assyria, 23, 25, 35, 38, 39, 41, 43, 44, 58, 59, 63, 85

—— II., king of Assyria, 58, 79

—— III., king of Assyria, 4, 79, 93-99, 106

—— IV., king of Assyria, 80, 103

—— V., king of Assyria, 111

Shamash, sun-god, 36

Shamash-bêl-utsur, viceroy, 58

Shamash-mudammiq, king of Babylon, 81

Shamash-shum-ukin, king of Babylon, 139, 140, 143, 144, 146, 155

Shamash-tsululushu, ancestor of Sennacherib, 3

Shamshi-Adad I., king of Assyria, 23, 39, 43, 44, 46

—— II., king of Assyria, 23, 38, 39, 41, 42, 43, 44

—— III., king of Assyria, 39, 41, 44, 47

—— IV., king of Assyria, 24, 44, 45

—— V., king of Assyria, 46

—— VI., king of Assyria, 58, 79

—— VII., king of Assyria, 99-102

—— B., king of Assyria, 38

Shamshi-ilu, Tartan, 104

Sharezer, son of Sennacherib, 130

Shar kishshâti, title, 46, 57, 62, 65

Sharrukîn, *cf.* Sargon I., king of Assyria, 39, 40, 41

Sharru-ludari, king, 141

Shaushka=Ishtar, 11

Shauskash, goddess of Mitanni, 11

Shem, son of Noah, 11

Shereshe, city, 72

Shiana, city, 95

Shinar, land, 1

Shinigsha, 88

Shubari, peoples, 53, 60, 62, 64, 71, 72, 155

Shunaia, 89

Shupri, land, 86

Shupri, land, 136

Shutur-nankhundi, king of Elam, 118

Sibate, 90

Sibi, general of Mutsri, 113

Sibir, king of Babylon, 88

Sidir, city, 138

Sidon, city, 91, 96, 102, 125, 137, 140, 143

Sieni, king in Nairi, 73

Silar, Mount, 100

Sillu, city, 138

Sillua, city, 138
Siluna, Mount, 102
Simaki, Mount, 87, 88
Sindjar range, 81
Singani, district, 59
Sinmuballit, fifth king of First Dynasty of Babylon, 42, 43
Sin-shar-ishkun, king of Assyria, 151, 152, 154
Sin-shum-lishir, king of Assyria, 152
Sinukhtu, province of Tabal, 116
Sipirmena, district, 87
Sippar, Sippara, city, 3, 42, 77, 82, 107, 118, 128, 134, 136, 144, 149, 152
Sirgani, city, 103
Sirku, 82, 84, 89
Sivan, 3rd month, 104
So = Sibi, q.v., 113
Standard inscription, 83
Sû, Mount, 87
Sua, river, 92
Su-abu = Sumu-abu, q.v., 37
Subbi-luliuma, king of Hittites, 53
Subnat, river, 85
Sugagi, city, 61
Sugi, 73
Sugia, 86
Sukhi, land, 74, 77, 84, 85, 90, 99
Sulili, king of Assyria, 37, 39, 102
Sulumal, king of Malatia, 108
Sumer, land, 65
Sumerian, 7, 8, 9, 10, 11, 33, 149
Sumu-abu, first king of First Dynasty of Babylon, 37, 38, 40, 43
Sumu-la-ilu, second king of First Dynasty of Babylon, 37, 38, 41, 42, 102
Sumu-li-el = Sumu-la-ilu, q.v., 37

Sumu-lili = Sumu-la-ilu, q.v., 37
Sunbai, district, 100
Supri, 89
Sûru, land, 9, 82, 84, 85, 88, 89, 93
Susa, city, 143, 145
Sutarna I., king of Mitanni, 54
—— II., king of Mitanni, 54
Suti, people, 51, 60, 62, 63, 117, 118
Synchronous History, 24, 47, 48, 56, 57, 68, 69, 77, 78, 80, 81, 101
Syria, land, 9, 35, 47, 50, 94, 96, 102, 107, 108, 110, 111, 112, 116, 143, 146

Tabal, land, 96, 99, 100, 116, 117, 119, 123, 124, 136, 141, 142
Tabit, city, 59, 89
Taharqa, king of Egypt, 139, 140, 141
Taiki, city, 63
Tala, Mount, 74
Tamesu, city, 138
Tammaritu, king of Elam, 143, 144, 145
Tanutamon, king of Egypt, 141
Tarbilu, city, 61
Tarbisi, city, 14, 130
Tarkhulara, king of Gamgum, 108
Tarsus, city, 5, 96, 123, 124
Tartan, title, 30, 59, 96, 97
Tartar, river, 81, 97
Tashmetum, goddess, 150
Taurla, district, 100
Taurus, range, 97
Tela, 86
Tell-el-Amarna, place, 49, 50, 55, 56

Tell-el-Amarna tablets, 49, 50, 51
Temeni, city, 103
Teshri, 7th month, 106
Teshup, Mitanni god, 11
Teumman, king of Elam, 142 143
Teushpa, king of Gimirri, Thebes, city, 140, 141
Third Dynasty of Babylon, see Kassites, 52
Thothmes I., king of Egypt, 51
—— III., king of Egypt, 51, 52, 55
—— IV., king of Egypt, 54, 55
Tiglath-pileser I., king of Assyria, 24, 25, 44, 45, 69, 71-78, 80, 85, 93
—— II., king of Assyria, 79
—— III., king of Assyria, 58, 79, 80
—— IV., king of Assyria, 4, 30, 105, 106-111, 115, 116, 134
Tigris, river, 12, 13, 14, 62, 63, 64, 84, 88, 89, passim
Til-abnâ, city, 90, 91, 99
Til-kamri, city, 107
Timnath, city, 125
Tirhakah, king of Ethiopia, 36
Trilingual inscription of Darius, 16
Tsaltsallat, river, 61
Tsilli-Bêl, king of Gaza, 126, 137
Tsimirra, city, 113
Tugdamme, king of Gimirri, 136, 147
Tugrish, land, 46
Tukulti-apil-esharra, see Tiglath-pileser
Tukulti-Ashur, king of Assyria, 67
Tukulti-Ashur-atsbat, 87

Tukulti-Ninib I., king of Assyria, 25, 58, 64, 65, 66, 69, 71, 78, 85, 129
—— II., king of Assyria, 81
Tulili, 88
Tulliz, city, 143
Turnat, river, 87, 100
Turuki, land, 62
Turushpa, land, 109
Tushkhan, city, 86, 88
Tushratta, king of Mitanni, 11, 53, 54
Tutammu, king of Unqi, 108
Tuzchurmati, place, 12
Tyre, city, 4, 36, 91, 96, 102, 108, 109, 111, 125, 137, 138, 139, 140, 141

Ualli, king of Mannai, 147
Uda, 92
Ukin-zêr, king of Chaldæa, 110, 111
Uknu, river, 107
Ulâ, river, 143
Ullubu, city, 108
Ullusunu, king of Mannai, 115
Ululai, king of Babylon, 111
Umalia, 92
Umildish, state, 115
Umman-manda, people, 155
Umman-menânu, king of Elam, 129, 135
Unasagusu, king of Sidir, 138
Unqi, 108
Ur, city, 9, 13, 32, 118, 119, 135, 143, 144
Urartu = Ararat, Armenia, land, 96, 97, 98, passim
—— Urartai, people, 108
Urikki, king of Quê, 108
Urmia, lake, 97, 98, 114
Urrartinash, city, 72

Urtagu, king of Elam, 136, 142, 143

Urume, place, 72, 86

Usanate, 95

Usana-khuru, prince of Egypt, 138

Ushpia, *cf.* Aushpia, 11

Ushu, city, 146

Van, lakes, 97, 109, 115

Vannic, culture, 97

Varuna, Mitanni god, 52

Waite, king of Arabia, 146

West Semitic, 39

Winckler, Professor H., 53

Yemenite, people, 114

Zab, river, lower, 13, 69, 73, 75, 77, 87, 100, 134

—— upper, 13, 14, 64, 84

Zaban, river, 69, 100

Zabdânu, brother of king of Babylon, 90

Zabibi, queen of Arabia, 108

Zaddi, city, 99, 100

Zamba, 92

Zamûa, land, 84, 86, 87, 88

Zamri, 87

Zanqî, city, 69

Zarpanît, goddess, 55

Zaza-bukha, city, 88

Zidqa, king of Askelon, 125

Zikirtu, land, 115

Zikurrat, temple stage tower, 13, 41, 121

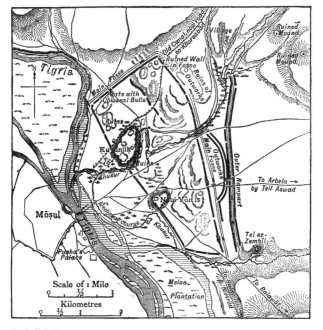

Labels on map:
Ruined Mound
Village
Ruined Mound
Old Canal now dry to Khorsabad
Ruined Wall in Fosse
Tigris
Main Fosse
Gate with Colossal Bulls
Ruins of Outworks
Ruins
Kuyunjik
Ruins
Khusur
Outworks
Main Fosse
Outer Rampart
To Arbela →
by Tell Aswad
Mōṣul
Ancient Course of Khusur
Nebi Yunis
Tel ez-Zembil
Pasha's Palace
Scale of 1 Mile
½
Kilometres
½
2
Melon Plantation
To Nimrud
To Baláwát

Camb. Univ. Press.

MAP OF NINEVEH.

Reproduced from *The Encyclopædia Biblica* by kind permission of
Messrs A. & C. Black.

MUSHKI R. Euphrat

Malatia

TABAL

Amedia

KIRK

Tig..

KHILAKKU

KASHIARI RA..

Tarsus

QUE

Carchemish

Haran

Zanjirti

Arpad

Aleppo

BIT

ADINI

R.Habor

Hamath

R. Orontes

Armad

R. E...

QE

KHINGANI

LEBANON

Damascus

Sidon

L. Tiberias

Tyre

Samaria

Joppa

Ashdod

Ammon

Jerusalem

Askelon

Moab

Gaza

Edom

.... border of Ashurnatsirpal III

—·—·—·—·—   ,,   Shalmaneser III

><><><><><   ,,   Shamshi-Adad VII

— — — — —   ,,   Adad-nirari IV

MAP
OF
THE ASSYRIAN EMPIRE

Camb. Univ. Press.

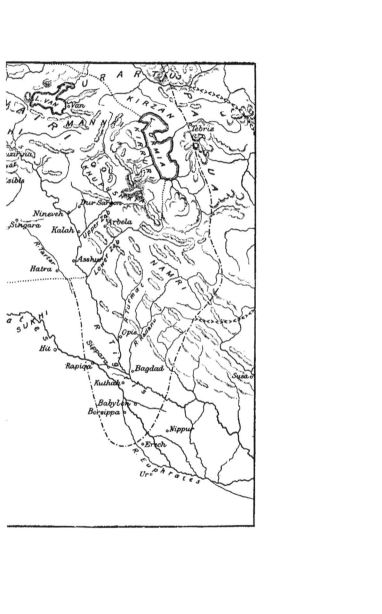

www.ingramcontent.com/pod-product-compliance
Ingram Content Group UK Ltd.
Pitfield, Milton Keynes, MK11 3LW, UK
UKHW042143280225
455719UK00001B/59